Praise for *What to Ask*

"*What to Ask* cuts through the clutter of customer data noise and guides us squarely into their hearts and minds where we can help discover the unspoken needs and desires they've yet to articulate. If you are competing in a space clamoring for insights about your customers, read this book. Twice. And slowly."

> **—Ron Carucci, Managing Partner, Navalent; bestselling author of *To Be Honest* and coauthor of *Rising to Power***

"*What To Ask* provides an enlightened view of the customer insight challenge that every single business today struggles with. And it delivers to-the-point, non-academic, no bullshit methods and guidance to address it."

> **—Dennis Sparks, retired Director of Global Supply Chain at Pfizer, board member at the University of Iowa's John Pappajohn Entrepreneurial Center**

"*What to Ask* is a must read for business leaders and decision makers at all levels and in every industry and an invaluable resource for entrepreneurs who are seeking to innovate and differentiate in emerging markets or in existing markets where current solutions no longer meet customers' needs."

> **—Tom Trone, retired global marketing executive at John Deere; Entrepreneurial Instructor at The University of Iowa**

"*What to Ask* is just *what we need* right now in the customer insights and marketing domain. Superior customer understanding is the new battleground for companies to gain a sustainable competitive advantage. This smart, practical guide leverages behavioral science to help you help customers *reveal* what really drives their decision-making, so that you have a real shot at impacting it."

> **—Elys Roberts, CEO & Founder, BEESY**

"A very thought-provoking look at how to better understand your customers. This book is packed full of fresh examples and practical case studies. Simply wonderful!"

> **—Richard Shotton, Founder, Astroten UK; author of the bestselling book *The Choice Factory***

"A must-read guide for anyone who wants to know what their customers or employees *really* want. This is an excellent, contemporary reference manual for people measurement and all the foibles of human nature that go with it, brought to life in a fascinating and memorable way."
—**Patrick Fagan, Co-Founder and Chief Science Officer, Capuchin Behavioural Science; Lecturer, University of London**

"This book will help sharpen your customer focus. Incredibly immersive yet practical, it skips all the vague theories and delivers an immediately applicable method to shift organizational mindsets around customers and what they need now."
—**Steve Blank, Adjunct Professor, Stanford University; Senior Fellow, Columbia Business School; Father of Modern Entrepreneurship; author of *The Startup Owner's Manual***

"This is the best title of any marketing book. And the contents more than live up to the promise. It is a masterclass in learning to uncover the decisive distinctions and paradoxes in human behavior, which most businesses overlook to their cost."
—**Rory Sutherland, Vice Chairman, Ogilvy UK; TED Global Speaker, author of *Alchemy: The Surprising Power of Ideas that Don't Make Sense***

"I teach every entrepreneur that they must know their customer better than their customer knows themselves. This is the first book that I've read that shows you exactly what that means and how to do it."
—**Gino Wickman, Founder, EOS Worldwide; author of *Traction* and *Entrepreneurial Leap***

"In this insightful, entertaining and practical book, Andrea gives hugely useful and valuable frameworks to ensure the questions you ask give you the answers you need to drive business success."
—**Richard Chataway, author of *The Behaviour Business*; CEO, BVA Nudge Unit UK**

"Customer insight is more important than ever. *What To Ask* explains cogently and practically how to understand customer needs in a world where technology creates the illusion that it's 'all in the data.'"
—**Martin Reeves, Chairman, BCG Henderson Institute; author of *Your Strategy Needs a Strategy* and *The Imagination Machine***

WHAT TO ASK

Also by Andrea Belk Olson

No Disruptions: The Future for Mid-Market Manufacturing

The Customer Mission: Why It's Time to Cut the $&% and Get Back to the Business of Understanding Customers*

WHAT TO ASK

How to Learn What Customers Need but Don't Tell You

ANDREA BELK OLSON

Matt Holt Books
An Imprint of BenBella Books, Inc.
Dallas, TX

BenBella Books, Inc.
10440 N. Central Expressway
Suite 800
Dallas, TX 75231
benbellabooks.com
Send feedback to feedback@benbellabooks.com

BenBella and *Matt Holt* are federally registered trademarks.

Printed in the United States of America
10 9 8 7 6 5 4 3 2 1

Library of Congress Control Number: 2021057355
ISBN 9781637740774 (hardcover)
ISBN 9781637740781 (ebook)

Editing by Katie Dickman
Copyediting by Ginny Glass
Proofreading by Jenny Bridges and Sarah Vostok
Indexing by Amy Murphy
Text design and composition by PerfecType, Nashville, TN
Cover design by Brigid Pearson
Cover image © Shutterstock / jiris
Printed by Lake Book Manufacturing

To my late father, Darwin. May we always be learning.

CONTENTS

Introduction   xi

How to Use This Book   xix

CHAPTER 1   Ways We Seek to Understand   1

CHAPTER 2   Customers Don't Know What They Want   17

CHAPTER 3   Data as a Security Blanket   35

CHAPTER 4   The Influence of Mindsets   47

CHAPTER 5   Customer Centricity vs. Customer Ownership   63

CHAPTER 6   The Impact of Company Culture   75

CHAPTER 7   Customer Action Learning   87

CHAPTER 8   Shifting Mindsets and Learning What to Ask   95

CHAPTER 9   Monetizing Customer Discoveries   119

CHAPTER 10   Creating Customer Strategy Scorecards   131

Epilogue   145

Acknowledgments   149

Bibliography   151

Index   175

INTRODUCTION

*How do we find out what our customers really
want?*

—Every Business Leader

Just take a spin through the Google machine, and you'll find millions of ways to discover what customers want. Go interview them. Send out surveys. Implement process X. Use method Y. Create customer personas. Define customer objectives. Yet even with all these methods at our disposal, the struggle to capture truly valuable and actionable insights persists.

Just take the story of the Sony Walkman.[1] Way back in the winter of 1999, Sony conducted a focus group for a new yellow Sport Walkman.[2] They assembled a group representing their diverse customer contingent and asked, "How do you like this yellow Walkman?" The reception was great.

"I love that yellow color—so sporty!"

---

1. Admit it: you had a Walkman. Or a Discman. Or at least an old-timey MP3 player.

2. It's a mobile audio cassette player, for all you Gen Z folks out there.

"Man, I would rather have a sweet yellow Walkman than a boring old black one."

Sony was thrilled with the positive input and offered participants a free Walkman on their way out. They could choose either a traditional black edition or the sporty yellow one. Everyone picked the black Walkman.

This is the ongoing conundrum: what customers say they want doesn't match their behaviors or voiced intentions.

Two Mentalities

Customer feedback is typically regarded in one of two ways. First, as a necessity. Want to create another product to sell? Ask the customer what they need. Think you have a good idea? Get the customer's opinion. When we apply their input and outcomes fall short,[3] we turn around and blame the customer.

"They told us they really wanted this feature. Why aren't they using it?"

"Customers said they wanted this product, but sales are going nowhere."

Or second, as a hassle. Customer feedback is completely disregarded or ignored because we believe we already know what customers want. Applying the Steve Jobs mentality, we develop and launch our ideas because "we know their needs better than they do." This approach seldom results in generating revolutionary innovations, aside from the tiny handful of well-known exceptions, like Apple or Tesla.[4]

---

3. Sound all too familiar?

4. These companies are unreasonable standards to be upheld to. They are the exception to the rule.

We Want Certainty

More often than not, customer feedback isn't about discovery, but about certainty. We use it as some type of justification for why an investment of time and resources will generate growth. But to have good certainty, you need great predictions. It's clear we continue to fail on delivering great predictions. This is no surprise, as tried-and-true methods often cause us to misinterpret customer intent and misunderstand customer context—the two most important insights to uncovering and exposing unique growth opportunities. Instead, we use flawed information to reinforce our existing perceptions rather than exploring how customers tick.

So how do we come to terms with our polarized mentalities and our voracious need for unwavering certainty? It starts with becoming more cognizant of our own misconceptions about customer needs, perceptions, and human behavior.

Distorted Thinking

Brand research routinely claims that people who are aware of communications from brand X are more likely to buy that brand. This is frequently used as evidence to validate the idea that communication drives sales. However, the causality runs the other way: buying brand X makes you more likely to notice its communications. People notice and remember the brands they know well and like. Recognition is the effect, not the cause.

Even though this misconception[5] has been well known for decades, it's still used to justify communication effectiveness. It isn't unique, as our thinking can become distorted when we fixate on what's measurable rather than what's useful. This includes giving superficial data precedence over deep insights.

---

5. The Rosser Reeves fallacy—named after the famous 1950s adman.

For instance, suppose a customer unsubscribes from a mailing list. Typically, they're asked to answer a single question indicating why they are leaving. We capture this information, draw a conclusion, and consider the job done. But was their reason even listed among the choices? If so, did this singular data point *really* provide a complete understanding of their perceptions and actions?

People Are Complex

We frequently assume customer needs are easily defined, and their responses will directly reflect those needs. This is rarely, if ever, the case. Capturing and interpreting feedback is a subtle, nuanced art.[6] When we oversimplify our questioning and overcleanse response options, it shapes feedback into neat little boxes, but dramatically hinders any useful interpretation of it.

The most valuable customer feedback is often qualitative. Yet qualitative data isn't clear. It's inherently vague and untidy. It doesn't deliver black-and-white insights. It's hard to measure. Surveys, questionnaires, and polls can help you learn about what a customer supposedly thinks at a moment in time, but those tools are not effective at helping you predict their future intent and behaviors because they lack context. Specifically, those circumstances and interrelated conditions that influence their responses.

Why Bother?

So should we even bother asking customers what they think? It's a reasonable question, and some organizations simply don't. A former global chief marketing officer at Cirque du Soleil, Mario D'Amico, once remarked: "How can people tell you what they want

---

6. Just try figuring out what your significant other wants or needs. Sometimes, it's not just about what they say.

if they haven't seen it before? If we ask them what they want, we'll end up doing *Swan Lake* every year!"

He makes a great point. Even the most innovative companies know you cannot implicitly trust customers to tell you what your next innovation should be. And no matter what businesses do to strengthen their survey methodologies, sometimes, customers may simply put little effort into their responses, or struggle to provide insight beyond a superficial tweak or two.

For example, you can ask customers the most important factor in selecting an insurance policy, and they'll provide the standard answers: cost, service, experience, and so on. However, if you ask them what they paid when they last made a claim or for details about their recent policy experience, they go blank. Having no answer means their survey responses aren't the sole reasons for their decisions—they're just the most mentally convenient ones.[7]

Sometimes we even create internal barriers to insulate ourselves from customer feedback, including things like:

- giving sales reps sole access and control of customer relationships.
- deeming marketing as the official interface to the customer.
- creating corporate policies restricting direct customer communications due to legal or public relations concerns.
- believing customers don't want to be asked for their feedback.[8]

So why capture customer input if it doesn't provide useful insights, is too hard to implement, or generates only self-validating information? Because it's essential to truly understanding customer mindsets and behaviors. And there's a new way we can acquire better, more actionable customer knowledge without moving heaven

---

7. And we're all a bit mentally lazy at times.

8. These are all real examples.

and earth.[9] A simple, effective method for putting yourself in your customer's shoes. One which doesn't require tons of people, costly third-party research, or experts to guide you through a convoluted process. You'll find in the coming chapters how to easily uncover customer needs and get your entire organization—including the cynics—on board with the value of customer feedback.

A Fresh Perspective

It seems everyone claims they're an expert. But there are all kinds of experts. Experts who have years of traditional schooling and numerous degrees. Or those who have cut their teeth moving through the ranks of some global consulting firm with a name that oozes credibility. Maybe they wrote a book or two and built a recognizable name through the speaking circuit and notable media exposure.

Yes, these are wonderful people, many of whom have incredible knowledge and practical experience. But unless they've dealt with obstinate, myopic bosses, the exhaustion of internal politics, the impossible task of meeting unattainable goals while being woefully under resourced, or the tediousness of navigating bureaucracy designed to insulate those who create little organizational value, do they really understand how to design and translate processes and methodologies into something you can truly use? No. Only someone who has lived those realities can.

Someone who started a company with a friend, $10,000, and no experience. Someone who helped build that company over ten years to $20 million and fifty employees, having to learn everything through trial by fire. Someone who moved into designing and leading a $400 million global organization's transformation strategy, dealing with the ins and outs of corporate politics, posturing, and

_____

9. If you want to skip ahead on this subject, go to chapter 8.

power struggles. Someone who expanded into academia, heading a specialized program for a Big Ten university, navigating organizational hierarchies, bureaucracy, and regulatory limitations. Someone who founded a nonprofit organization, learning how to build and execute a program with only volunteer support. Someone who built a second company because they couldn't tolerate watching organizations repeatedly make the same mistakes, simply due to misinterpreting customer needs. That someone is me.[10]

I created this book with the same practicality and piss and vinegar that carried me through these challenges. The intent is to provide a comprehensive tool set not only for better understanding your customers, but also for understanding all the elements impacting your ability to apply that knowledge in your organization effectively.

Most processes, concepts, and methodologies are presented in a bubble, coupled with a waterfall of case studies from multibillion-dollar companies where organizational leaders supported and funded change efforts. These big, audacious case studies don't reflect the common business—they are the 1 percent. They are unicorns. They show how things can be done perfectly, but in perfect scenarios. Most organizations don't have all the necessary pieces in place, nor are they able to acquire them. In short, it isn't reality— it's the exception.

You'll find throughout this a clear, pragmatic approach to understanding mindsets and perceptions, how to shift them, how to use them to see unseen opportunities, and how to influence them to create actual change. Make no mistake, this isn't a paint-by-numbers process or a step-by-step recipe where you pour in the right ingredients and out pops the fruitcake. What you will get is

---

10. I don't like talking about myself much, so you won't find more details in this book. Dig into LinkedIn if you want to learn more.

a sharp-edged, straight-to-the-point guide[11] on how to go from status quo to customer-centric, starting with the history of customer understanding, transitioning to getting in the right mindset, and ending with a methodology for uncovering hidden needs.

But why now? Because it's long overdue. Organizations cannot flourish without understanding the ever-changing needs of their customers. Without an intimate knowledge of customers' fears, motivators, challenges, and goals, how can new innovations and differentiators arise?

---

11. The key word is *guide*. You'll have to apply critical thinking and effort. If you're looking for an autopilot solution, this might not be for you.

HOW TO USE THIS BOOK

By now, you've skipped the introduction.[1]

But read this.

This book is designed in thirds.

The first third sets the foundation for getting you and your organization in the right headspace, helping you understand those influencing factors that inhibit efforts to shift your company's focus on the customer. It is essential to absorb and internalize the obstacles you're facing, as any attempts at change without knowing these will fall short.

The second third talks about the how—specific strategies, methods, and tactics for gathering, understanding, and applying customer insights super effectively. You're free to jump directly into these chapters anytime. Depending on your circumstances, it might make sense to skip to the nitty-gritty. If you're leading a small business, for instance, you might not have to worry about dealing with an entrenched culture, and you can just flip things on a dime, so go for it.

The last third is all about translating customer insights into the language of business: how to convert knowledge into measurable returns. Regrettably, most business books don't include this

---

1. I do it all the time.

critical part, giving you only reams of case studies, and leaving you to your own devices to connect the dots.

Then there's the epilogue. This was included for a single purpose—giving you the inspiration and confidence needed to take what you've learned here and implement it. We often read inspiring works, but rarely do they become something we use in our companies. If you don't apply this new knowledge, it's not worth much.

You'll also find little Easter eggs[2] throughout the footnotes. I find footnotes boring and rarely ever read them. So it was high time to make them better. Some footnotes will provide additional clarification to specific terms and phrases, but many will be a running commentary, including a bit of humor and snarky quips. There are some people who pick up a book and want to get to the meat—those specifics that they can immediately apply to their organization without lengthy author narration. Others want to peek inside the personality of the writer, hear stories, and connect with them like a friend. No matter your preference, this book allows you to choose your own reading experience.

Hope you enjoy.

---

2. Not as cool as in the movies, but fun nonetheless.

Ways We Seek to Understand

The ways of yesterday are not enough to understand the world of today.

—King Zhao

A clay tablet dating back to 1750 BC sits in the British Museum. It documents a customer complaint about a shipment of copper. According to the interpretation, the shipment was the wrong grade of metal and took too long to arrive.[1]

Ever since there were products and services to sell, there have been customers. Customers are the lifeblood of every organization.[2] Because customers fuel growth, there have been many different approaches over the decades to discovering and capturing better customer insights.

---

1. Some things never change.

2. There are some organizations who don't believe this, truly.

In the early 1900s, businesses collected customer information via face-to-face interviews or mailed questionnaires. By the late twentieth century, telephone and email surveys became major mechanisms. Now, organizations are consuming instant online reviews, social media commentary, and live chat questions. But is that information being leveraged for new innovations or simply utilized for here-and-there adjustments to internal processes?

Collecting Data or Understanding People?

Companies are spending incredible amounts of resources, time, and money to create huge customer data pools. Some are applying this information effectively, but others are simply amassing a collection that sits on the proverbial shelf.[3] Today's level of information accessibility has brought about a kind of factory mentality, where organizations generate as much data as possible about customer interests, behaviors, and needs. Yet companies need to examine if this data factory is actually producing new, revolutionary insights or if data gathering itself has become the objective instead.[4]

Understanding customers means understanding people.[5] This requires *learning* what influences their behaviors and decisions. It makes logical sense this should be done through direct engagement, observation, and interaction, yet organizations continue to try to substitute data for discussions.

Why? Because understanding people is not as easy as it sounds. Existing processes only address parts of this challenge. We need to

---

3. How many reports and studies has your company run over the years, and where is that data now?

4. Be honest. Do you really read and parse through all that customer data?

5. You can't get around this. Customers are people, and I challenge you to find an exception.

shift our mentality. We need to start applying a fostering approach through which customer relationships are formed to uncover not only hidden needs but also the contexts in which those needs occur. People are more than trends, scores, and rankings—and data alone can't deliver authentic insights without context.

> ### What to think about through this chapter:
>
> * How our relationships with customers have changed over time
> * Why traditional research methodologies fall short
> * The three different types of customer knowledge

A Quick History on Customer Relationships

Customer relationships have transformed significantly over the decades. Until approximately the mid-1800s, we lived in the simple trade era—a time when everything was built by hand, and only in limited supply. Commodities were incredibly valuable, and people only consumed what they needed.

The Industrial Revolution spawned the production era (1860s through the 1920s), shifting the focus to increasing efficiency, attaining economies of scale, and operating on the assumption that demand exceeds supply. The belief was products themselves were the source of need, or simply stated, if you build it, they will come. Limited energy was put toward understanding customer needs. Efforts instead centered on raising awareness of the product's existence.

As markets became more saturated and competition increased, the sales era of business began (1930s through the 1940s), bringing aggressive door-to-door sales tactics. The goal was to acquire every possible sale, maximizing transaction frequency with as many customers as possible.

The marketing era (1950s through the 1990s) then emerged to address the challenge of competing solely on price and availability. Often coined the disruption era, advertising and telemarketing were designed to persuade customers to buy products using aesthetic, emotional, and social influences. This era also spawned the field of market research, shifting the mentality from mass production to customer satisfaction. By finding holes in the market, businesses could capitalize on the unserved and underserved needs of customers.

Only in the relationship era (early 2000s through today) did the concept of customer centricity—building genuine connections between company and customer—come to the forefront. Because it costs approximately five times more to obtain a new customer than to maintain an existing one,[6] organizations now seek to maximize the value of each customer interaction. Using multiple touchpoints, they capture information to help customize and personalize customer experiences.

Enter the New Tech

Now that we can capture customer data from virtually anywhere, at any moment in time, the challenge becomes how to track, sort, store, and digest it. In response, a tidal wave of platforms has entered the scene, helping efficiently capture and manage this information, including customer relationship management (CRM) software like Salesforce, HubSpot, Insightly, Microsoft Dynamics, and Sugar. Or customer communication tools, such as Mailjet, Constant Contact, Adobe Campaign, Mailchimp, and many more. Other technologies including chatbot systems, help-desk systems, and social media management tools are also in the mix. The tech stacks alone are

---

6. If you don't believe me, just calculate your customer acquisition cost (CAC) versus your retention cost.

overwhelming. According to Chiefmartec.com, there were over eight thousand different marketing technology platforms on the market as of April 2020, and that number continues to rise.

Methodologies to Fill the Gap

Data collection is one thing. Drawing clear, actionable insights from that information is another. Why even have data if we can't translate it into unique differentiators and new revenue streams?[7] This is where everybody struggles. It's all good and well to know *what* actions customers are taking, but the hard part is understanding *why*. So we turn to tried-and-true methodologies to supplement our knowledge and help us decipher customer needs, archetypes, experiences, and satisfaction further.

However, most of these practices haven't changed in decades. Customer personas were developed in 1980. The jobs-to-be-done theory in 1992. The customer journey in 1998. Net promoter scores in 2003. While useful in their own ways, these methods can be misleading if misapplied, cumbersome to implement, or simply insufficient in drawing out new insights. It's high time for a new approach,[8] but let's first evaluate some of the most popular tools in the box.

Net Promoter Score Is a (Really) Flawed Metric[9]

The net promoter score (NPS) is widely considered a benchmark of the customer pulse. You know the method: "On a scale of one to ten, how likely is it that you would recommend our company/product/service to a friend or colleague?" If a customer rates their

---

7. Yes, you can sell data, but do you really want to be in that business?

8. If you are already on board, skip to chapter 8.

9. Hear me out.

likelihood a nine or ten, they are a promoter. If they rate between one and six, they are a detractor. Passives fall at a seven or eight. A company's official net promoter score is the percentage of promoters minus the percentage of detractors. In essence, the higher your score, the better.

There's a simplicity and elegance to that single question. It's easy to track and easy to measure. But a score alone doesn't provide insight on what gave rise to a customer recommending or not your company, product, or service. Without understanding the scoring context, there is no conceivable way to drive improvement.

In 2019, the *Wall Street Journal* published "The Dubious Management Fad Sweeping Corporate America," covering the increasing popularity of net promoter scores. The article discussed the number of times NPS were cited in earnings calls by fifty S&P 500 companies, noting, "More than four times as many mentions and nearly three times as many companies, compared to five years earlier." This reflected the belief that one simple number could predict growth. Companies obsessively tracked it, changed business models and systems around it, and redesigned customer experiences to drive up scores. Leaders were often promoted or fired based on them. The belief even turned into a measure of organizational culture, where employees ranked their likelihood to recommend the company as a place to work to friends and family.[10]

However, NPS has an inherent flaw—nine doesn't equal ten.

Why does that matter? Because there is a big difference in the behaviors of actively engaged, indifferent, and disengaged customers. Gallup research in 2019 found actively engaged customers delivered a 23 percent premium in share of wallet, profitability, and revenue over an indifferent customer. The same study also uncovered 90 percent of customers who rated a company a nine were indifferent to that organization.

---

10. I think employees inherently know what happens if they score as a detractor.

Another Gallup study from 2018 examined 24,000 customers across 2,734 financial institutions. Customers who gave a ten score were five times more likely to be actively engaged with their bank than those who gave a nine. Those who gave a ten were also twice as likely to be extremely engaged. In the same study, only 31 percent of customers who scored a nine on NPS were extremely satisfied with their bank, compared with 80 percent of customers who score a ten—a forty-nine-point difference.

Besides inflating the percentage of true promoters, NPS underrepresents detractors. The same study revealed 20 percent of customers who scored a seven or below were fully disengaged with their bank. Net promoter scores may be a comforting metric, but it can give organizations a false sense of security. Customer satisfaction is multifaceted and can be influenced by a wide range of factors. NPS provides no insight as to why someone gives a particular score.

A rating can be rather useless if you don't understand the motivation behind it. Without the why, there is no way for a company to determine how to improve a product or service, or what direction to move. Without understanding the why, organizations spend excessive time and energy trying to guess what went wrong and how to fix it.

Gaps in the Customer Journey Map

The whole idea of customer journey mapping[11] is to create a visual representation of customer experiences with a company from the customer perspective. There isn't one generic customer or one generic journey. Different customers inherently have different needs and, therefore, experiences. They have different moments

---

11. A customer journey map is a diagram that illustrates the steps your customer(s) go through when engaging with your company, whether it be a product, online experience, retail experience, or service, or any combination thereof.

when these experiences are good, bad, or in between. Even if two customers take the same journey, they will have very disparate perceptions of it.

Therefore, to fully understand the customer journey requires a full comprehension of their unique goals, frustrations, emotions, feelings, and intentions. It's a time-consuming grind to examine the entire customer experience rather than just interaction touchpoints. Often, however, organizations will get a whole bunch of people in a room, document their internal process, and call it a customer journey map, without ever actually talking to customers.[12]

A friend of mine recently shared how talking with customers upended their understanding of the journey map. "A few years ago, we had each employee watch customers use our product for an entire day. It was the most embarrassing and most valuable day I think I ever spent. So much about what we thought about the customer journey was wholly wrong. On top of that, some of the key measurements we were looking at (such as when customers abandoned the SaaS product) were incredibly misleading. Sometimes the root cause was a loss of confidence at an earlier step, but the abandonment didn't happen immediately, causing us to believe the problem was when the abandonment happened versus when the confidence was lost."

Optimizing the customer experience is critical for organizational growth, as PricewaterhouseCoopers found in a recent study. They found 86 percent of buyers were willing to pay up to 18 percent more for a great customer experience. A Walker Information study also projected that, by the end of 2022, customer experience will overtake price and product as a key brand differentiator.

---

12. This happens way too often. I've seen it firsthand.

Yet disappointingly, customer journeys have mostly become a fancy term for product, service, or interaction design,[13] essentially outlining how customers find you, compare options, make a purchase, receive a product, and done! Creating the map becomes the organization's objective over gaining experience insights.

Given the effort required to create a comprehensive, company-wide customer journey map that outlines every stage and step across every customer archetype and channel, it's almost impossible for an organization to go beyond just scratching the surface. You only get a general view of the shoreline with a journey map. While they can uncover areas of experience misalignment, they don't give necessary weight to external criteria including customer mindset and context.

They are also susceptible to journey bias—where companies define the journey that best suits the organization rather than the customer. Without supporting qualitative research, organizations often lose sight of how one touchpoint fits the customer's overall goals and objectives. Maps then devolve into modest optimizations of internal processes rather than creating new, value-added differentiators for customers.

The Genericism of the Customer Persona

Customer personas began as user personas in 1980 when Alan Cooper, a pioneer tech developer, designed a series of profiles for people using his software interface. Later, famed ad agency Ogilvy turned the concept into customer personas, intended to better understand target audiences in the form of a single page brief, outlining perceived interests, behaviors, and preferences. Yet personas, again and again, turn into a character invention exercise, in which organizations make up imaginary customers with fictional

---

13. Think UX (user experience design) and UI (user interface design).

wants, without ever conducting any real research, talking to real people, or collecting real data.[14]

Personas are typically filled with generic customer needs and concerns, making them useless for addressing unique customer problems. For example, a major software company identified one of their persona's frustrations as "slow download times" and "data crashes." How are those specific to one persona? These frustrations apply to every living person on the damned planet.

Or consider two different customer personas for an online job board—job posters and job seekers. The same person could fit both personas over time. Someone posting jobs may also seek a change in their career. At that point, they'd also become a job seeker, so what unique insight does the persona deliver? Persona profiles may correlate to stereotypes, but they typically don't identify distinct challenges.

Customers can also have different or similar problems, regardless of their age, occupation, location, status, or educational background, although these characteristics are always featured as key elements of personas. Different people may fall under the same persona and behave completely differently under different circumstances, such as whether they are under a time crunch or not. Thus, personas alone deliver little meaningful insight, and can cause organizations to pursue customer assumptions that have no basis in reality.

Yet, personas can serve a purpose. Sales teams need to understand who their target audience is, their general interests, and their pain points. Customer personas are a good cheat sheet. They give frontline salespeople a basic framework for evaluating leads and opportunities. But personas are simply a starting point. Without

14. Clearly, there's a pattern here of using tools as a substitute for customer discussions and exploration.

real insight, from real customers, they're just hypothetical arche-types filled with hypothetical insights.

The Overengineered Jobs-to-Be-Done Theory

The jobs-to-be-done theory (JTBD) is an approach to understanding customer choice and behavior. The "job" is the progress a customer is trying to make. The customer, in theory, hires and fires products and services to complete that job efficiently and effectively.

JTBD was popularized by Clayton Christensen's books on innovation and disruption, primarily his 2016 *Competing Against Luck*.[15] His basic argument is you will create something innovative by focusing on the job the customer needs to be done, especially if it isn't being done by another product or service on the market.

The JTBD methodology emphasizes capturing qualitative cus-tomer data. Christensen argues, "You need to get out of the building and talk with customers to uncover the true jobs those custom-ers need to do."[16] However, this piece is never defined.[17] There are no clear specifics to the customer research process. Consultants have tried to expand on it but provide little detail beyond "con-duct customer interviews to define the core job to be done." Author Anthony Ulwick outlines the JTBD theory in his book *Jobs to Be Done: Theory to Practice*, in an eighty-four-step approach he calls outcome-driven innovation, where customer research is described in only a single step. This brings to light the fact that there's no clear method to capturing qualitative customer research.

---

15. There's some debate about when JTBD actually came about, as it has changed a bit over time.

16. As a side note, Steve Blank coined the phrase "get out of the building and talk with customers."

17. Really.

The other challenge with the JTBD framework is the influence of bias. A great example of this is the story of Abraham Wald, a Hungarian mathematician. During World War II, the United States was looking to better armor and equip their fighter planes. They would examine the planes that returned from battle and observe where the most damage had occurred.[18] Adding armor was not only expensive but also made the planes heavier, made them less maneuverable, and caused them to use more fuel.[19] So the military presumed the "job" was whatever areas were being damaged the most, that's where armor should be. But Wald had a different idea. If planes were returning with damage to certain areas, it meant those areas weren't critical. It was evidence of survivable damage. He hypothesized the undamaged areas of planes are where armor should be increased, because planes damaged in those areas never made it back. He was right.

Jordan Ellenberg describes a similar scenario, noting, "If you go to the recovery room at the hospital, you'll see a lot more people with bullet holes in their legs than people with bullet holes in their chests. But that's not because people don't get shot in the chest; it's because the people who get shot in the chest don't recover."[20] What underlies both bullet-hole problems is a phenomenon called survivorship bias—a cognitive error in which only the "survivor" data is examined, without considering the information that could be gleaned from those that didn't survive.

This bias influenced how the military viewed the job to be done. They believed to improve plane survivability, the job was to add additional protection to the most-hit areas of the plane. Wald's perspective was unbiased, helping him to see the job as protecting

---

18. Essentially, they counted the number of bullet holes per square foot.

19. Too much armor is a problem and too little armor is a problem.

20. From the book *How Not to Be Wrong*.

areas where the aircraft was unscathed, but if hit, it would cause the plane to be lost.

It's a different way to approach the same job, but Wald's way of looking at it enabled him to identify a solution that was counterintuitive to the military's perspective. In short, different jobs can be interpreted differently, and defined differently by different people. Having a common, unbiased understanding of the customer job is essential for identifying innovative solutions. The JTBD framework doesn't explicitly tackle how to do this outside of a dozen or so guidelines, which fundamentally reiterate "think about the job from the customer's perspective."

The Process and Research Problem

While these methodologies are useful in certain times and places, they all carry notable downsides. Company leaders are motivated by quick, clear, and measurable outcomes. Lengthy or abstract processes are frequently viewed with a high degree of skepticism and often seen as pollution to productivity.

This creates a negative perception of customer exploration and research overall. Something that takes weeks or months and a lot of human power to implement but results in only a stack of observations and vague conclusions is a major deterrent to organizational executives who see the need to learn from customers but despise the process.[21]

Since these approaches have delivered less-than-stellar outcomes in the past, companies are not eager to get back on board. We may agree that gathering customer input is important and agree to implement a survey here and there, but won't commit to embedding a customer insight exploration mentality as a long-term part of the organization's ecosystem and culture. This leads

---

21. You might even dread the process yourself.

to information apathy, where customer input is simply used for internal validation and appeasement instead of conducting true customer exploration and challenging status quo perceptions.

Unless there is a more effective way to uncover and generate new and differentiating insights, the practice of customer research will continue to fight an uphill battle for recognition, respect, and adoption. Therefore, we need to break down the complexity of what constitutes customer information, how to better capture and analyze it, and how to connect it directly to positive business outcomes. The first step is gaining a better understanding of the different types of customer knowledge available.

Understanding Types of Customer Knowledge

Customer knowledge is fundamentally the combination of observed, captured, and gleaned information from interactions between a customer and a company. There are three basic types of customer knowledge:

1. **Knowledge *about* Customers**—anything captured through customer transactions and interactions[22]
2. **Knowledge *for* Customers**—anything captured identifying customer wants, needs, and challenges
3. **Knowledge *from* Customers**—any expertise gathered from customers as they utilize your products and/or services

These three types of knowledge are distinctly different. Companies nowadays collect *about* customer knowledge through every possible digital mechanism: online forms, transaction records, and purchasing data—you name it. This knowledge is usually the most attractive to company leadership, as it can be quickly translated into new revenue opportunities. For example, things like purchase history

---

22. You've likely got this data already.

can be leveraged for cross-selling activities. Yet for the obscene amount of intelligence hoarded, it is rarely exhaustively dissected.

Organizations capture *from* customer knowledge to validate[23] existing perceptions or to justify a course of action. This includes information about how a product or service is used, including customer-designed workarounds and unorthodox applications. Derived from customers who obtain their own unique expertise when utilizing your products or services, this knowledge can be applied directly to things like new features and add-ons. Regrettably, this information is typically used to develop a new enhancement or two rather than create deep customer partnerships.

For customer knowledge is all about wants and needs. This includes feedback on experiences, perceptions, big-picture problems, and challenges. This knowledge is the hardest to obtain but the most valuable, as it uncovers hidden opportunities for differentiation and innovation. For this knowledge, we usually ask customers, "What can we do better?"[24] and anticipate a myriad of surprising and unique ideas.[25] However, creating success here is not about just asking customers *any* questions, but the right ones. Experts don't clarify what those questions are[26] or how to interpret the answers. They tell you to keep it open-ended and not to ask leading questions or too many questions. Talk less and listen more. It's advice that reads like a horoscope—it can apply to anything and everything.

For customer knowledge can be the difference between minor improvements and epiphanies. But no customer research effort will be effective without first determining what you seek to

---

23. Or invalidate. Always a possibility.

24. And receiving answers that range from "nothing," at worst, to "improve customer service," at best.

25. Which never come.

26. This book will address these specifics in chapter 8.

understand. Only then can you identify the customer knowledge you need or whether you already have the answers at hand.

Why We Need Better Insights

You can apply all these tools and methodologies and still not know who the hell your customers are. The point and purpose of these tools is to help you gain knowledge—the deeper the knowledge, the better. If you're only using these methods to gather superficial insights or satisfy an internal need from the boss, it doesn't really matter what tool you use or how you go about gathering data.

Why? Because the objective in those instances isn't about learning; it's only about checking a proverbial box. The goal is to show there was an attempt to gain insights and deliver a shiny document with a lovely series of pie and bar charts and a handful of cherry-picked customer comments. We need to change the objective, and existing tools don't help shift our mindsets to make that happen.

If you take nothing else from this chapter, remember to focus first on the question you're trying to answer, not what insight you want to gather or how you want to gather it. Forget about the tools and processes until you know this. As Lewis Carroll alluded to in *Alice in Wonderland*, if you don't know where you're going, any road will take you there.

2

Customers Don't Know
What They Want

The customer's perception is your reality.
                                    —Kate Zabriskie

Every evening, I ask my husband what he wants for dinner. He never knows. Even when provided with a list of options, he defers to an ambivalent "whatever you want" reply. At restaurants, after scouring the menu like it's a legal contract, he defaults to the safe and familiar steak or burger.[1] These aren't tough decisions, yet everyone struggles with these types of things at one time or another—sometimes more often than we'd like.

Now consider a bigger, more complex decision. Choosing a plumber for a bathroom remodel. Buying your first home. Deciding on a new inventory management platform for your company. These are *way* more sophisticated decisions than choosing dinner. You must understand a broad spectrum of information, which also

---

1. He's really not as bad as I'm painting him to be.

needs to be gathered, sorted, and weighed to make your selection. This isn't an easy task.

Or take the scenario of selecting a personal financial adviser. Unless you have some background in finance, you likely have minimal knowledge of what makes a good adviser. I mean, it's not something you do every day, like making the morning coffee or walking the dog. So you start by asking friends and family for recommendations. Maybe you get a couple of individual names or suggestions of well-known companies. You might stop here because, "I know my friend Steve wouldn't steer me wrong. I always trust his suggestions."[2]

For argument's sake, let's say instead you hop on the good old internet and conduct a bit more research. You learn about other professionals in the local market, examine their specialties, identify their offerings, and, of course, compare prices. Now you have a matrix of information, but the choice isn't crystal clear. Maybe you have multiple priorities, and no single option fully covers the spread. Or maybe you're unfamiliar with industry-specific terminology[3] and don't fully understand what you're even evaluating. Unlike the simplicity of a dinner selection, this education and evaluation requires significant time, attention, and mental effort.[4]

The problem is that people are often lazy, overwhelmed, or scared about making decisions. Maybe it's unclear the reward for acting is worth the payoff. Maybe there are too many options to choose from, making it difficult to select one. Maybe there is a fear about the consequences of a choice. For all these reasons and more, we often avoid or dodge complex decisions. It's just human nature. However, by understanding the role emotions play in decision making, we can guide those decisions more effectively.

---

2. Believe me: don't trust Steve.

3. Like the meaning of *fiduciary* or what a Series 65 license is.

4. Sometimes that dinner choice can take just as much mental effort.

What to think about through this chapter:

- How emotions can overpower logic
- How cognitive biases influence decisions
- Where customer decisions, feedback, and predictions intersect

What Influences Decisions

Portuguese American neuroscientist Antonio Damasio made a groundbreaking discovery during his research in the early 2000s. He studied people with damage to the part of the brain[5] where emotions are formed and stored. Essentially, these people functioned normally but were incapable of feeling emotions. Surprisingly, they also had one other thing in common—they couldn't make decisions.[6] They could describe what they were trying to do in logical terms but found it almost impossible to make even simple choices, such as what to eat.[7]

Emotions are the dominant influence on the decisions we make, the actions we take (or don't take), our perceptions, attitudes, judgments, and interpretation of the world around us. Harvard professor and researcher Gerald Zaltman found that pure rationality, practicality, and objectivity only represent about 10 to 20 percent of our decision making. Just consider those decisions you make when you feel hungry, angry, lonely, or tired.[8] Emotion wins 100 percent of the time.

---

5. The amygdala!

6. No, this is not my husband's condition.

7. Arguably, maybe it is.

8. Or God forbid, some combination of more than one.

Yet the traditional methods we've used for decades to help customers make better decisions overemphasize the influence of rational thinking. Jonathan Haidt, in his book *The Righteous Mind: Why Good People Are Divided by Politics and Religion*, states, "The mind is divided, like a rider on an elephant, and the rider's job is to serve the elephant. The rider is our conscious reasoning—the stream of words and images of which we are fully aware. The elephant is the other 99 percent of mental processes—the ones that occur outside of our awareness, but actually govern most of our behavior."

Enter the Concept of Behavioral Economics

If emotion dominates logic, how can we effectively understand and influence customer rationale?[9] This is where behavioral economics comes in. It has only recently entered the business nomenclature, gaining notoriety from the work of Nobel Prize winner Daniel Kahneman and his 2013 *New York Times* best seller *Thinking, Fast and Slow*.[10] It aimed to change the way we think about decision making by integrating insights from psychological research with economic science.[11] In short, behavioral economics is the study of judgment and choice, and how to influence them.

Our choices are never made in isolation. They're impacted by things we're conscious of (our environment, our budget, etc.) and things we're unconscious of (errors in our patterns of thinking). Those unconscious errors—referred to as cognitive biases—occur when our brains try to simplify information processing. Information overload sucks, so we aggressively filter. This mental

---

9. Or lack thereof.

10. I won't go into his book here, but recommend you pick up a copy.

11. Also known as "the dismal science," coined by Thomas Carlyle in the nineteenth century. Fact of the day!

skimping[12] results in going with what feels right, while unintentionally applying faulty logic.

Cognitive biases affect everyone's choices, judgments, and perceptions. With hundreds of scientifically recognized biases, it's hard to know which ones may be impacting a customer's decision-making processes. However, there are eight biases that frequently affect customers' decisions. Let's look at each along with how organizations play a role in influencing them.

Bias #1: Curse of Knowledge

Christmas is coming, and Jim's four-year-old sister, Jane, is ecstatic about Santa Claus. She wrote multiple letters to Santa and decorated sugar cookies for his upcoming arrival. As a twelve-year-old, Jim can't understand why his sister doesn't realize their parents are the ones leaving gifts under the tree. Because Jim knows Santa isn't real, even though he once believed he was, it's difficult for him to understand Jane's innocent perspective. The curse-of-knowledge bias colors our ability to relate to the less-informed perspectives of others, and even recall our own previously-held naivete.

How It Applies

Being well-versed in our organizational bureaucracy and industry jargon, we tend to overlook the obstacles and frustrations customers face when navigating our business domain. Internal terminology, acronyms, protocols, and red tape are things we assume customers understand about our language and processes. We create tools and concoct procedures meant for customers but which fit *our* mindsets. We are blind to the customers' vantage point

---

12. Often referred to as heuristics. Find more on this in chapter 4.

because, once we understand something, it's hard to imagine what it was like not knowing it.

I took my seventy-eight-year-old mother to get a new cell phone plan. Explaining nuclear fission to a fourth grader might have been an easier task.[13] And not because my elderly parent is less than tech savvy, but because the person helping us was *too* knowledgeable. Every question posed to my mother about data usage, 5G access, and hot spots, I had to translate into a language she could understand. "Mom, a hot spot is like a cable box—when you turn it on, your computer has access to the internet, just like your TV has access to different stations." When customers don't understand, they can't make effective decisions.

Bias #2: Status Quo Bias

Consider a major college that utilizes a digital platform to manage courses campus-wide. One of their business department programs doesn't use the system. Attendance, homework, grades, and communications are all cobbled together in a variety of spreadsheets, documents, and email folders. When the idea was proposed to utilize the campus platform, the team was all for it. Yet after it was rolled out, they continued to use the old processes. Why? Status quo bias is the tendency to prefer the current state of affairs. It was easier and faster to utilize the old methods because they were familiar, requiring less mental effort than learning a new system.

How It Applies

In our organizations, we see the same challenges and follow the same processes day after day. This immersion helps us accept and

---

13. I still love you, Mom.

utilize processes that would be considered clumsy and complex to someone unaccustomed to them. A relatable example is Mac versus PC. Depending on which you use, it can take significantly more mental effort and time to conduct the same task on the competing system.

Customers will resist change, even if it's to their benefit. The global pandemic forced massive changes in customer behavior virtually overnight. In banking, people who were used to stopping by the lobby to deposit a paycheck had to learn how to make the transaction through a phone app.[14] Even though this option has been available to most bank patrons for years, resistance continued because of unfamiliarity and unfounded fears. Comfort, consistency, and confidence in the status quo overpowered the willingness to try an alternative approach.

Take any other change which shifts from the status quo, whether switching from a cable provider to a streaming service or simply using a QR code to view food options rather than a paper menu at a restaurant. While some people will be early adopters to change, many people will struggle with accepting that the benefits of change logically outweigh the efforts of change.

Bias #3: Maslow's Hammer

A hammer isn't the ideal tool for every job. It's great for hanging a picture frame but useless for repairing a broken television or unclogging your toilet.[15] Even so, a person with only a hammer will figuratively try to fix everything using their hammer, without

---

14. I had been going into the lobby each time, even though I use my banking app all the time. I wanted to build a relationship with my bankers in case of future needs. I digitally deposit now, which is convenient, but impersonal.

15. I guess it depends on how you use it—it would be possible to unclog a toilet with a hammer, though the unclogged toilet would be left in pieces.

considering other tools. We prefer to utilize what we have rather than seek something different. The bias describing this tendency was named after Abraham Maslow, who in 1966 stated, "I suppose it is tempting, if the only tool you have is a hammer, to treat everything as if it were a nail."

How It Applies

When I injured my back by lifting a heavy suitcase, I went to see an orthopedic surgeon who recommended herniated disc surgery without first considering nonsurgical treatment options. Surgery was their hammer.[16] Our brains attempt to work efficiently by referring to past solutions, without giving the current problem much thought. It tends to function on autopilot. We apply previously used methods and tools to a seemingly similar problem, instead of evaluating the problem on its own terms.[17] This narrows our ability to keep an open perspective on customer challenges and reduces our capacity to creatively problem solve.

When we are oriented to a particular solution to a problem, we become blind to alternative approaches. Customers think in the same way. They may ask for specific features and options but are drawing from what is already established and familiar. It's akin to the frequently used Henry Ford quote, "If I had asked people what they wanted, they would have said faster horses."[18]

---

16. I've found all surgeons tend to be this way. They just love to cut people open and dig out the baddies.

17. There's a companion article I wrote on my blog on this subject, titled "Is Time-Bound Memory Causing You to Be Stuck in the Status Quo?"

18. Yeah, I know there's debate on whether he actually said this, but it's a good quote nonetheless.

Bias #4: Bikeshedding

We seem to spend an inordinate amount of time on the inconsequential. Then, when an important decision needs to be made, we have little time to devote to it. This is *bikeshedding*, where we tend to give excessive weight to trivial issues. It was named after a metaphorical example of a management committee's decision to approve the design of a nuclear plant with no deliberation, but then conduct a heated debate on what color the company bike shed should be.

How It Applies

Simple problems are easy to tackle. Complex challenges take a lot more brainpower. We often deflect, circumvent, or put off these decisions. If our to-do list consists of the grocery store, laundry, and filing taxes, we tend to prioritize picking up lettuce and folding sweaters because they are simple and menial. We feel more comfortable and accomplished working on the effortless.[19]

Let's say a customer is evaluating a variety of enterprise software platforms. Instead of assessing the features and functions of each, they focus on trivial items in the contract documentation. The customer might not be well versed on the technology underpinnings, so they avoid asking questions. Instead, they fixate on the irrelevant. This avoidance results in customers spending an inordinate amount of time on decision points that have little to no impact on outcomes.

---

19. This can also be interpreted as "yak shaving"—any useless activity which, by allowing you to overcome mild challenges, allows you to solve a larger problem.

Bias #5: Context Effect

Picture yourself basking in the sun on a sandy beach, with the smell of salt in the air and the ocean water tickling your toes. A waiter strolls up and offers you an ice-cold bottle of your favorite beer. You're more than happy to pay the ten dollars the resort charges.[20] But if you ran down to the grocery store, finding that same beer at the same price would be considered highway robbery. The context effect is the influence environmental factors have on customer perceptions.

How It Applies

The perceived value of something will change dramatically depending on context. Context can mean many things, including physical environment, social environment, and situational environment (such as time of day or mood). What customers think about a product or brand depends on the context in which it is viewed and experienced.

Consider a time when you waited in line while being in a hurry. Did the experience seem to take longer than normal? Was it more frustrating than usual? Was it different from your previous experiences, or did it simply feel that way?[21] People often see themselves as independent thinkers, but we are all heavily affected by context.

Bias #6: Google Effect

Imagine you're reading a book, come across a peculiar word, and google its definition. A few days later, you can't recall what it means.

---

20. No, it wasn't a craft beer. Just a typical domestic.

21. Be honest.

The Google effect[22] is the tendency to forget information readily available online. The internet has become a part of our daily lives, making access to information so seamless we find ourselves looking up the same information repeatedly rather than committing it to memory. This goes for other information accessible via phones or computers as well. Are your friends' phone numbers memorized or simply stored in your contacts list?

How It Applies

According to a 2015 study by Microsoft, people on average lose concentration after eight seconds[23]—highlighting the effects of an increasingly digitalized lifestyle on the brain.[24] Companies who spend extensive effort in curating a distinct path for customers to follow will find it circumvented with a quick search.

For instance, a company may spend hundreds of hours crafting user guides for their software, pointing customers to a document repository on their website in an effort to control the brand experience, only to find them going unused. Customers instead are googling homegrown how-to videos on YouTube. The Google effect enables customers to seek the path of least resistance, often taking organizations out of the decision set if critical information is hard to find, unhelpful, or simply inaccurate.

Bias #7: Perceptual Salience

We know apples and carrot sticks are nutritious, but they're quickly forgotten when cruising through the supermarket and seeing an

---

22. Also known as "digital amnesia."

23. Common estimates of the attention span of healthy teenagers and adults range from five to six hours; however, there is no empirical evidence for this estimate.

24. The average attention span for the notoriously ill-focused goldfish is only nine seconds.

alluring box of cookies.[25] The packaging design sways you to make a choice eliminating all considerations for healthiness. Perceptual salience arises from vivid contrasts between items and their surroundings. In essence, we tend to spotlight things that are unique or emotionally striking, even though they may have no beneficial impact on the decision being made.

How It Applies

We are predisposed to identify prominent and distinctive details, which can lead us to ignore potentially vital pieces of information. If customers see few meaningful differences between various alternatives, they will default to the easier choice and select the first alternative they notice, rather than making the effort to conduct a more thorough comparison.

Alternatively, if we're familiar with something, it can create a preference over alternatives. Say your friends convince you to go to a new Vietnamese restaurant in town. You're a bit apprehensive, as you've never eaten Vietnamese food before.[26] You flip through the menu and find fried rice—a safe bet. The known outweighs the unknown, because an unfamiliar dish may put you at risk of not enjoying your meal.

Bias #8: Surrogation

Pretend you're a manager tasked with increasing customer satisfaction. Your performance is measured by these ratings, so you begin to equate high satisfaction scores to actual satisfaction. While a high score may be indicative of satisfaction, the score itself doesn't create it. This myopic focus on scores can usurp efforts or activities

---

25. Snickerdoodles all the way.
26. Try it. You'll love it.

that genuinely improve satisfaction. Surrogation is the tendency for people to lose sight of objectives and give undue importance to what represents them. Or according to Goodhart's law, "when a measure becomes a target, it ceases to be a good measure."

How It Applies

We all know the story of Wells Fargo, where employees opened over three million deposit and credit card accounts without customer consent to meet the goals of the organization's cross-selling strategy.[27] When employees are rewarded for meeting target numbers over the objective itself, counterproductive behaviors come into play.

Think back to the last time you were asked to rate your experience a ten on a satisfaction survey because customer service claimed, "Anything less than ten, we consider failure."[28] That pressure may have caused you to provide an artificially high score and hold back constructive criticism. These tactics tend to lower a customer's actual satisfaction, but surrogation causes us to continue using them.

What We Know and What We Think We Know

Back in 2007, Universal McCann conducted a global study with ten thousand people about portable digital devices. At that time, the first iPhone was on the verge of a worldwide release. Surprisingly, the researchers concluded products like the iPhone weren't something desired in affluent countries, specifically stating, "There is no real need for a convergent product in the United States, Germany,

---

27. What a shit show.

28. I'm sure you can think of an instance right now.

and Japan." They theorized people wouldn't be motivated to replace their existing digital cameras, cell phones, and MP3 players.[29]

This type of incongruence between predictions and reality has caused many organizations to conclude customers don't know what they want, and research doesn't bridge the gap. Companies conduct survey upon survey, leading to new products not selling, and new features going unused. Yet just like Maslow's hammer, we are trying to apply one tool for multiple challenges. We don't consider things like cognitive biases or dig deeper into the customer context.

In the Universal McCann study, people were asked how much they agreed with the statement "I like the idea of having one portable device to fulfill all my needs." There was a significant difference between those who completely agreed with the statement in Mexico (79 percent) versus the United States (31 percent). Given this feedback, you'd have reasonably assumed that Americans weren't interested in a phone that was also a camera and music player.

However, when the iPhone got closer to launch—when people heard about it in the media, read user reviews, and saw articles about this revolutionary device—preferences began to change. When first questioned about their interest, people had no frame of reference for what a phone-camera-email-music-player was.[30]

Prediction versus Preference

Universal McCann accurately reported what they found. They fell short, however, by overestimating the degree to which customers

---

29. We all know how that turned out.

30. Why did the people in Mexico have a bigger preference, as they didn't know what an all-encompassing product was either? Because they didn't have as many products to potentially replace. Universal McCann wasn't completely wrong, but their conclusion was inherently just an assumption about behavior.

could predict their future actions. There is a big difference between prediction and preference. Asking a customer if they prefer option A to option B is one thing. Asking them to predict future wants and needs will generate misleading outcomes if taken at face value. The very definition of prediction is what someone thinks will happen. History has its fair share of those who claimed to predict future actions, from Nostradamus to your daily horoscope. When we try to predict future customer behavior through research, the result is a slightly educated guess.

Recently when having a beer with friends, we discussed a well-publicized murder trial. We recounted the suspect being questioned at their workplace and en route to the police station. "I would have stated my innocence right out of the gate," one said. "There's no way I wouldn't have gotten pissed. I'd be furious, to say the least." While they proclaimed to know exactly how they would behave in the situation, the accuracy of those predictions can't be proven—at least not without a real-world test.

Maybe we'd freeze up from the shock of being accused of something so heinous. We might be so wrapped up in processing the situation we'd have a hard time even talking. Or we might remember all those *Law & Order*[31] episodes and try to avoid saying anything that could be used against us in a courtroom. Our ability to predict what we'd do is fundamentally an opinion. This fact about predictions leaves organizations trying to translate vague musings of surveys and studies into not-so-predictive documents. The gap in the Universal McCann study wasn't the data but the lack of inductive reasoning.

---

31. Bonk, bonk!

Don't Trust First Impressions

If the objective is to improve customer predictions, we need to move beyond the superficial glimpse our basic data-collection methods provide. This means not relying on first impressions. We need to craft multiple possibilities, also known as inductive reasoning. In short, this involves forming a series of hypotheses from specific information you've learned, observed, or experienced, and then determining whether they are true or false.

For instance, if Harold is a grandfather and he is bald, would you deduce all grandfathers are bald? No, since you know that not all grandfathers are bald. Even though all premises here are true, inductive reasoning allows you to determine the conclusion to be false. In short, inductive reasoning is about questioning the conclusions you draw from data and using observations and insights to get closer to the truth rather than simply sticking to your initial assumptions and impressions.

This method of reasoning is critical for the interpretation of customer input. Instead of simply accepting our data as fact, we use our own experiences, observations, and knowledge to create other hypotheses. We can then use this for deeper exploration, uncovering flaws and overlooked opportunities within our data assumptions.[32]

A great way to do this is through the Delphi technique.[33] Developed at the beginning of the Cold War to forecast the impact of technology on warfare, the process encompasses selecting subject matter experts, who review the data and draw a series of hypotheses and their detailed reasoning behind them. By going through multiple cycles of review and discussion, a consensus can emerge

---

32. And assumptions make an ass out of "u" and me.
33. Often called the Estimate-Talk-Estimate method.

on the best hypotheses drawn from the data rather than the first conclusion out of the gate.

So it's not enough to ask for customer feedback and call it a day without considering biases, perceptions, and experiences. If you take nothing else from this chapter, remember our cognitive biases and emotions are the biggest influence on our decision making. We are not inherently logical creatures.

3

Data as a Security Blanket

Strategy without tactics is the slowest route to victory.
Tactics without strategy are the noise before defeat.

—Sun Tzu

When an organization is experiencing success, it's not easy to understand why there's any need for change. However, when it comes to our customer data collection habits, it's high time we cease our autopilot gathering and storage of information. I mean, how relevant is the number of retweets your posts had in 2015 to the performance and growth of your business today?

Organizations have long been living the ethos of acquiring everything. Form submissions, personal information, clicks, time on the website, page views, attendance, likes, you name it. "Just collect it all and we'll work out what to do with it later." The danger of this real-life hoarding is we are becoming data rich and insight poor. More data is not the answer.[1]

---

1. There are companies I know who spend gobs of money on data collection and studies—and they do nothing with it.

Data hoarding diverts often scarce resources that could be better applied elsewhere. If customer insights are the proverbial needle in the haystack, more data simply makes the haystack bigger, and the needle much harder to find. Take the example of finding terrorist activity. Security expert Bruce Schneier framed the issue plainly: "Piling more data into the mix makes it harder, not easier . . . the last thing you want is to increase the amount of hay you have to search through." There's an opportunity cost in looking at the wrong data and not knowing the right questions to answer. In short, too much of a good thing can be a bad thing.

Don't get me wrong. Data can be valuable, but gathering more data shouldn't become a distraction or, worse, the focus itself. Anything added to the pile should be guided by a clear purpose. What questions are we trying to answer that our current data doesn't? How does this new data reduce uncertainty or provide more clarity?

There is comfort in having "all the data." Organizations that have been collecting data for years may feel an emotional attachment to this legacy information, even if it's no longer relevant. It's silly. Most companies operate in fast-moving environments where critical insights come from what's happening now. Why not focus on *now* data? Even retail behemoth Walmart relies on only the last four weeks' worth of customer data to run their daily merchandising activities.

Data itself has little value unless something can be gleaned from it. Most companies struggle to understand and effectively utilize the customer data they have, but they gather more. Yet when answers to critical business questions aren't found, they assume there was simply some magical, hidden gap in the data. This misunderstanding arises from the lack of clear goals and, more importantly, clear objectives.

The belief that data equals knowledge is a common misnomer. The ability to draw meaningful conclusions is when data becomes truly useful. Data is a collection of facts in raw form. Without context, data can mean very little. For example, *12012012* is just a sequence of numbers, but in the context of "this is a date," we can easily recognize December 1, 2012. Now we have transformed raw data into information.

In short, data given context becomes information. Information given meaning becomes knowledge. Knowledge given insight becomes wisdom. Wisdom given purpose becomes decisions. Therefore, we need to utilize our data to grow organizational knowledge and leverage that wisdom to drive action.

What to think about through this chapter:

- How misleading conclusions can be drawn from data
- Understanding the differences between data, information, and knowledge
- Why you need a Why and Wherefore Statement

Big Data and Spurious Correlations

A few years back, the concept of Big Data claimed to address the challenge of gleaning valuable customer insights. Big Data is now everywhere because of the growth of devices recording data, and the connectivity between those devices through the internet.[2] Praised as a transformative innovation, advocates claim it can crunch mass amounts of numbers to solve virtually any problem.

There are many great uses for Big Data, but everything has its downside. We don't have to look far to find major scandals.[3] Big Data systems *can* find subtle patterns in data sets, but they can't tell us which correlations are truly meaningful. As we know,

---

2. Remember that iPhone they thought nobody would buy?

3. Remember Cambridge Analytica?

correlation does not equal causation. However, we're hardwired to look for patterns,[4] and when we see lines sloping together in our data, it's hard for us not to believe there's a causal relationship.

Tyler Vigen, the author of *Spurious Correlations*, highlights this issue through a series of comical-yet-technically-correct line graphs showing how monthly US ice cream sales track in perfect parallel with forest fires, shark attacks, and even polio rates. Simply because ice cream sells more in the summer, there's no real correlation with an increase of shark attacks during the same period, but the data can cause us to perceive it.

In statistics, a spurious correlation is a mathematical relationship where two or more items or events are associated but not causally related. It can be due to either coincidence or the presence of another factor (seen or unseen).[5] In the case of increased ice cream sales and shark attacks, that other factor is temperature. Higher temperatures cause more of us to buy ice cream, as well as go to the beach for a swim.

Adding Data versus Adding Information

When organizations continue to gather customer data without rhyme or reason, without understanding why, and without clearly defining the problem that needs to be solved, no software or analysis tool will generate beneficial insights. Recent research[6] has found that as data sets grow larger, they contain significantly more arbitrary correlations. These correlations were proven to appear solely due to the number of items in the data sets.

---

4. Think perceptual salience.

5. Commonly called a "lurking variable."

6. Check out *The Hidden Risk of AI and Big Data* by Vegard Flovik to dig into this further.

Companies need to shift their thinking from adding data to adding information. More data does not equal more information— at least useful information. Data has a built-in bias. Social media, for example, is a rich source of data. During Hurricane Sandy, FEMA could gather crucial details from Twitter about people's whereabouts, conditions, and needs. Gathering more data from other social media sites, however, wouldn't add any information about those without power or internet access. In that case, it might require actual boots on the ground.

Before considering gathering new data, companies need to first understand their objectives, and then determine the type of information needed to address them. This starts with defining those objectives.

Back to Business 101

Executives are infatuated with goals. One CEO of a global manufacturing company[7] even stated their only goal was to increase sales. The prevailing belief is that to grow an organization, you need specific, measurable, actionable, relevant, and time-bound goals.[8] Yet they usually manifest as broad, generic, and unrooted in research. Things like "ensure success for enterprise customers," or "increase sales leads by 10 percent." When you establish bad goals, you get bad objectives.

An objective sets a specific and focused strategy to attain said goal. Bad objectives read like a to-do list. Most people create objectives as a target or aim rather than a strategic approach to solving organizational challenges. For example, an objective might be creating a customer loyalty program for the goal of growing customer retention. There's no clarity as to why this approach is preferred

---

7. Who shall remain nameless.

8. Though many supposedly SMART goals don't even meet this threshold.

over others and no specific parameters for determining success or failure (other than creating the program itself).

The Why and the Wherefore[9]

What sets successful organizations apart is understanding *how* their goals can be achieved. To truly understand and define the *how*, you must first understand *what*. The missing component is a Why and Wherefore Statement.

A Why and Wherefore Statement defines not only a problem to be solved and the perceived cause but also how you will go about trying to solve it.[10] This approach shifts the perspective from "things to do" to "problems to solve." For example, a traditional goal and set of objectives might take the following form:

Goal: Grow customer retention by 25 percent in the Millennial market.
Objectives: Conduct a video marketing campaign for at-risk customers. Create a rewards program. Develop a customer advisory board.

While these objectives may have merit, they are a shot in the dark. They are solutions to an undefined problem that is impacting retention. Has customer retention been declining only in this segment or in others as well? What is a healthy retention rate for our industry and offerings? What outside factors have been impacting retention rates, such as the entrance of new competitors or technologies?

_____

9. If you know what song this phrase is from, I'll buy you a beer.

10. Sometimes this is referred to as a problem statement in technical product-development circles.

A Why and Wherefore Statement is a situation-and-approach model, highlighting the information we know today, our assumptions on the cause, and our approach to validating or invalidating those assumptions. Using our example above, a Why and Wherefore Statement might take this form:

> **Why and Wherefore Statement:** Customer retention rates with Millennials have declined, creating a loss of $465k in revenue this year alone, which may be due to three new competitive products in the market (why), creating the need to examine how customers perceive and utilize our current offerings (wherefore).

Albert Einstein famously noted, "If I were given an hour to save the planet, I would spend fifty-five minutes defining the problem and five minutes solving it." Organizational goals are empty without a comprehensive understanding of the issues underlying them. A goal of growing customer retention by 25 percent might seem admirable, but without more context, we can't determine whether it's worth pursuing in the first place.

Data, Information, Knowledge, Wisdom

John Kelly, IBM's father of Watson, said 80 percent of data is untouched, meaning it's never actually used to make improvements or changes to the customer experience. No matter how much data or information you have on customers, it needs to be translated into action, something executable that can be tested, measured, and refined.

The more we enrich our data with meaning and context, the more knowledge and insights we get out of it, enabling better informed and data-driven decisions. Harold Geneen, author of the 1984 book *Managing*, stated, "When you have mastered numbers, you will in fact no longer be reading numbers, any more than you read words when reading books—you will be reading meanings."[11] Without action, there's little sense in gathering, capturing, understanding, leveraging, storing, or even talking about data. And action usually requires change.

Easy and Hard Changes

Change comes in all shapes and sizes. Small, transactional changes are easy—rework the usability of an application form, create a new feature on your website, add a new component to your product. These are low-hanging-fruit changes. Most companies use customer data for these types of tweaks all the time. Then there are big, gnarly changes, those which require major infrastructure, process, and cultural adjustments, and cost a lot of money, time, and even more concerning, effort.

For example, one US retailer found it could increase profits substantially[12] by increasing the time items were on the sales floor before and after discounts. Yet implementing the change would have required a complete reorganization of their supply-chain processes. It would have been a major undertaking with no guarantee[13] that the financial predictions would pan out. So they didn't do it. Without confidence in your data, there's little impetus to take on these massive, potentially high-risk changes.

---

11. A critical difference. The tricky thing about numbers is figuring out what they mean for you.

12. Was projected to increase by double digits.

13. Nothing is ever a guarantee.

Enabling Data Dissection

In the not-so-distant past, computers were only given to executives or engineers. But now everyone's got one, along with the essential tools and training to use it effectively. The same should go for data. Creating a data-empowered organization requires restructuring work processes and behaviors to enable employees to use data to make better business decisions.

A perfect example of this is 7-Eleven Japan, where operation field counselors (OFC) visit each of the company's 21,000 stores twice a week, helping salesclerks learn to use data effectively. They compare each clerk's hypotheses on what would sell during the prior week versus what sold. They discuss how to analyze customer data and how to improve performance for the next week. The OFC is a full-time position to which high-performing salesclerks can be promoted.[14]

Empowering your entire organization to understand, evaluate, and embrace customer data requires commitment. Commitment means investing time today to reap the benefits over the long term, just like French army general Hubert Lyautey (1854–1934), who instructed his gardener to spend the next day planting a row of sap-lings on his property. The gardener agreed yet advised Lyautey that that species of tree required one hundred years to fully mature. "In that case," Lyautey said, "plant them now."

Many companies talk a good game about being data driven, but when data is only accessible and understood by a select few, the effectiveness of that insight is inherently limited. By committing to an immersive and pervasive approach to using data across the entire company, you can capitalize on its value over the long term.

---

14. Elegantly brilliant, no?

Data versus Knowledge

Organizations don't need to just learn how to use customer data, but also how to look beyond the numbers. A great example of this skill in action is Netflix. The idea of giving viewers a digital catalog for streaming online not only killed video rentals but also made Netflix a cultural phenomenon, as viewers embraced a new way of getting their entertainment.[15]

In the very early days, Netflix didn't have original content, but they were obsessed with customer data and, more importantly, behaviors. They found 76 percent of viewers said watching multiple episodes of a great TV show was a welcome refuge from their busy lives. They also found the tipping point at which viewers actually got hooked on a show was never the pilot episode, but a few further in.

Netflix capitalized on these behavioral insights by developing a strategy to release all episodes of shows simultaneously instead of releasing them one at a time as had been done since the dawn of television. The term *binge watch* became the *Collins English Dictionary* word of the year in 2015. Their success came down to not only having data but also applying knowledge gained from that information. Since Netflix was able to look beyond the numbers, they were better equipped to address what customers were wanting.

While some companies can draw valuable knowledge from data, others can be misled. An energy company observed customer attrition correlated to the frequency of customers' Google searches for an energy supplier. They deduced from the numbers that online searches were responsible for 65 percent of churn.[16] Yet when they

---

15. Yes, I know there were other factors involved, but we won't delve into those here.

16. Ridiculous, I know, but they initially believed this was the problem. Remember spurious correlation?

examined customer behavior, it revealed their decision to switch providers was triggered by extensive competitor advertising and promotional pricing. Google searches were not the cause of attrition, as people had already made up their minds by the time they started searching.

So never pass on the chance to get more context about a problem. The more informed you are, the better your assumptions and data interpretations will be. If you take nothing else from this chapter, remember that data doesn't give you all the answers. It's how you interpret data that creates the aha moments.

4

The Influence of Mindsets

I skate to where the puck is going to be, not where it has been.

—Wayne Gretzky

The night before the space shuttle *Challenger* disaster on January 28, 1986, a three-way teleconference occurred between Morton-Thiokol Inc. (MTI) in Utah; the Marshall Space Flight Center (MSFC) in Alabama; and the Kennedy Space Center (KSC) in Florida.

The teleconference was organized at the last minute to discuss temperature concerns raised by MTI engineers, who had learned overnight temperatures for January 27 were forecast to drop into the upper teens. They had nearly a decade of data showing the shuttle's O-rings performed increasingly poorly when temperatures dropped below sixty degrees.

In addition, the forecast high for January 28 was in the low thirties. Shuttle program specifications stated unequivocally the solid rocket boosters (the two torpedo-looking devices on either side of the orbiter shuttle)—and all the other equipment for which MTI was the sole-source contractor—should never be operated below forty degrees.

Launch votes (go/no-go) had to be unanimous, not just a majority. MTI originally voted to hold the launch. They stated, "Based on the presentation our engineers just gave, MTI recommends not launching." However, MSFC personnel pushed back hard. MTI managers finally caved after going offline to "reevaluate the data." The MTI general manager, Jerry Mason, told Vice President of Engineering Robert Lund, "Take off your engineering hat and put on your management hat." Lund instantly changed his vote from no-go to go.

This vote change was incredibly significant. MTI had four managers and four engineers present on the call. All eight initially voted against the launch. After MSFC's pressure, all four engineers were still against launching, but all four managers were for it. In the end, they excluded the engineers from the final vote[1] because, as Jerry Mason said in front of the Rogers Commission in the spring of 1986, "We knew they didn't want to launch. We listened to their reasons, but in the end, we had to make a management decision."[2]

You could argue the failure was caused by poor leadership or poor decision-making. However, the shuttle catastrophe is a vivid example of how organizational and individual mindsets can produce devastating outcomes.

---

1. Idiotic decision.

2. This is what gives managers a bad name.

> ## What to think about through this chapter:
>
> - How fixed mindsets cause major problems
> - Why mental shortcuts affect our judgment
> - Why things that work in one place don't work in another

Fixed Mindsets, Catastrophic Outcomes

In the case of the *Challenger*, the team experienced the phenomenon of plan continuation error—the cognitive bias to continue a course of action, even in the face of changing conditions. Plan continuation errors have been recognized as a significant factor in many aerospace and maritime accidents.

A 2004 NASA study found aircrew exhibited this mindset in nine out of nineteen accidents analyzed. In the Torrey Canyon oil spill, one of the worst in UK history, a tanker ran aground when its captain continued with a risky course rather than accepting a delay. A study of 279 commercial airline approach and landing accidents (ALAs) found plan continuation errors were the fourth most common cause.

Mindsets aren't just beliefs or opinions. They orient our reactions and impulses. In the face of uncertainty, we tend to double down on existing courses of action, particularly when we have invested considerable time, effort, and money in them.[3] While the *Challenger* launch team had clear evidence and cause for change, their mindset was closed to information running contrary to their fixed objective—launching the shuttle on schedule.

---

3. This is often termed the "sunk-cost fallacy."

Think back to instances when you've heard in meetings, "Well, all customers are that way," or, "It's just one customer who thinks that." These generalities are based on mindsets, not actual observations or information. They materialize from cultures where assumptions are not challenged and where people haven't been pushed beyond their intellectual or emotional comfort zones.

Mindsets can influence all aspects of decision-making and customer understanding.[4] They can reinforce collective biases, mask blind spots, and create organizational immunity to change. Even if customers are demanding change, organizational mindsets can restrict the ability to make it occur.

Instead of using a comprehensive set of unbiased facts to form balanced judgments, we take mental shortcuts. Referred to as heuristics, we draw from our past experiences and knowledge to derive quick and easy conclusions. This makes sense, as it would be impossible to gather and evaluate every bit of information available before making any decision. Nevertheless, we can place too much trust in these mental shortcuts. They can cause us to overlook relevant details or make spontaneous decisions without a supporting rationale. Here are seven frequently overlooked heuristics which unconsciously shape organizational mindsets:

1. Unconscious Affinity

Unconscious affinity is the tendency to favor people who remind us of ourselves. We've all heard the phrase, "You remind me of myself at that age," and understand how that kinship can result in preference. In organizations, unconscious affinity can propel people to give someone an opportunity over another simply because of their similarities.

For example, we may unconsciously select team members for a project who are like us, and unknowingly dismiss perspectives

---

4. If you want to learn more about mindsets and perception, take a look at my TEDx talk, "Why Data Doesn't Change Minds."

from those in the group who are dissimilar. This can cause us to overlook information that may be incredibly valuable, simply due to our perceptions of the source.[5] This applies to customers as well, where we may value the feedback from certain groups or individuals that we better relate to over others we don't.

2. Self-Confirmation

Self-confirmation is our tendency to seek or notice information that supports our existing beliefs. If you've already made up your mind that a certain conclusion is the correct one, self-confirmation will have you valuing evidence supporting your perspective over information that doesn't. You may disregard useful feedback, dismiss unique approaches, and ignore ideas that conflict with your mindset.

Self-confirmation also can reinforce stereotypes we have about people. Take customer personas,[6] where archetypes are created to represent common traits of a target audience. Unintentionally, we can apply self-confirmation through the demographic characteristics we choose to define them, including things like name, gender, age, and ethnicity. Sharon, the fortysomething conservative soccer mom, drives a minivan. Trace, the twentysomething country guy, drives a pickup truck with his dog in the back,[7] and so forth.

3. Conservatism

Similar to self-confirmation, conservatism causes us to favor the familiar over anything new which may threaten our preconceptions. We tend to give more credibility to information that supports our existing beliefs, and weigh less heavily or dismiss information which runs contrary to them.

---

5. This also impacts diversity, inclusion, and equity.

6. Refer to chapter 1 for a refresher on this.

7. Or maybe in the front.

For instance, Nokia's upper management believed customers only wanted improvements to the technical features of their existing mobile phones. When middle management attempted to share new research revealing competitor smartphone offerings and newly voiced customer needs, it was completely dismissed. Instead of developing a new operating system which customers desired, Nokia stuck to their existing beliefs and created more models of their current phones. In six years, Nokia's market value declined by 90 percent, and they were eventually acquired by Microsoft in 2013.

4. Fundamental Attribution Error

Fundamental attribution error is our tendency to believe that what people do reflects who they are. This causes us to overemphasize personal characteristics, ignoring situational factors when judging others' behaviors. In other words, we tend to cut ourselves a break while holding other people fully accountable for their actions. For instance, if you've ever chastised a "lazy" employee for being late to a meeting and then turned around with an excuse for being late yourself, you've made a fundamental attribution error.

We can judge customers in the same way. Consider a customer who doesn't respond or ignores multiple email follow-ups. You might be inclined to form a judgment of their character based on this experience alone.[8] Yet their behavior may be due to other factors, such as emails getting caught in a spam filter or their internet being down for a week, both of which have nothing to do with the quality of their character.

---

8. You have at one point or another. Don't lie.

5. Mental Laziness

Mental laziness is the tendency for people to think and solve problems in simpler ways rather than in more sophisticated ones, regardless of their intelligence. Just as a cheapskate avoids spending money, the human mind tries to avoid spending excessive cognitive effort. This autopilot thinking diminishes our deductive reasoning and problem-solving skills.

For instance, let's say you own a restaurant and are thinking about adding a new item (sweet potato fries) to the menu. You survey customers on *whether* they like the idea. The responses are easy to understand: forty-four yes, sixteen no. You interview another set of customers about *what* they like about sweet potato fries. Some say crispiness, a few mention shape (e.g., waffle, traditional, thin cut, and so on), and others share preferences about dipping sauces and toppings (e.g., honey, cinnamon, and so on). Because open commentary is more difficult to assess, you weigh the first survey's data as more important, even though preference does not directly equate to purchase behavior.[9] Hence, you add sweet potato fries to the menu, but don't see them selling in droves. Why? You didn't consider all the purchase-influencing variables from the interviews, just the popularity of the idea from the simple survey.

6. Tribal Loyalty

Tribal loyalty occurs when group conformity takes precedence over alternative perspectives. It causes teams to minimize conflict and reach consensus without critical evaluation or discussion. This reduces your ability to remain objective, stay skeptical, and express contradictory ideas.

---

9. For example, those who said they preferred sweet potato fries may not be willing to pay an extra $1.50 upcharge for them.

Let's say you're meeting with colleagues, discussing the results of a customer feedback survey. As the manager voices their conclusion about the data, each of your colleagues agrees. Even though you have drawn a different conclusion and believe the group should go a different direction, you feel pressure (whether subtle or overt) to go along with the established position.

7. Intuition[10]

Your gut feelings can be right in those spur-of-the-moment situations when a lot of analysis isn't possible. A study published in *Nature Neuroscience* in 2008 documented people reviewing abbreviated videos of basketball players shooting free throws. Even before the ball left the players' hands, professional basketball players who watched the videos could consistently predict whether the shot would go in. Their predictions were significantly more accurate than the predictions of nonplayers. In other words, their experience created more accurate intuition.

Or take a small group of tight-knit colleagues who all work in a customer-facing department. They have consistent exposure to customer feedback and collaborate daily, sharing ideas, challenges, and experiences. They build an intuition—a predictability about customer requests and repeating issues. Their intuition is much more accurate than that of the department manager, who only periodically reviews summarized complaint reports.

---

10. Some people say intuition is a heuristic, while others argue intuition is made possible by heuristics. Either way, it's worth mentioning.

What Happens When We Take These Mental Shortcuts

A recent documentary highlighted a string of murders in West Yorkshire and Manchester, UK, between 1975 and 1980. Like the historic Jack the Ripper, thirteen women lost their lives to serial killer Peter Sutcliffe. It was one of the largest and most expensive manhunts in British history. The police were criticized for their failure to catch Sutcliffe, despite having interviewed him more than nine times throughout the investigation.

Early on, the police identified a pattern of attacks occurring in red-light districts. This single data point became ingrained in the force's mindset, directing the focus of the investigation. Jim Hobson, a senior West Yorkshire detective, told the press in 1979, "He has made it clear he hates prostitutes." However, many of the victims had no association with or history of prostitution. Instead of considering this inconsistency, the police either discounted certain murders as separate from the investigation or insinuated victims who fit the red-light district pattern had a history of streetwalking. It was determined this mindset delayed an arrest by years.

Renowned psychologist Daniel Kahneman explains these downstream impacts of mental shortcutting this way: "If we [see some elements] of a story, we construct the [most familiar] story we can out of those elements. And we're not really fully aware of what we don't know. For example, let's say I tell you about the leader of a nation and say she's intelligent and strong. Now, if I ask you at this point if she's a good leader, you already have an answer: she's a good leader. But now, I tell you the third word was corrupt. So, I hadn't told you anything about her character. You were not waiting. You took the information that you had, and you made [the most familiar] story possible out of it. That's how our minds work."

Kahneman points to our inherent desire to draw conclusions as quickly as possible. We don't wait. We don't consider what we don't know. We take information at face value rather than taking more time to understand the bigger picture and the possible flaws in our thinking. And this can cause us to pursue approaches which may not completely fit the circumstances.

The Ron Johnson Trap: Why Formulas Don't Work[11]

In June 2011, Ron Johnson, the man in charge of Apple's wildly profitable retail stores, a Steve Jobs acolyte, and a former Target executive, was hired to take the helm of the flailing JCPenney operation. He had an idea for a new kind of retail store and now had the chance to make it a reality. Johnson focused change in three key areas. First, end the use of constant markdowns and coupons, instead offering customers consistent pricing. Second, turn JCPenney stores into a destination filled with branded merchandise. Third, reduce private-label brands (even though they generated 50 percent of sales).

According to a 2019 article in *The Observer*, "This was radically different than the operating model J. C. Penney had been using for years. Johnson believed he could create a better customer experience for J. C. Penney's existing customers while attracting new ones. Attracting new customers was exactly what J. C. Penney needed. Executive leadership wanted to transform the company, and Johnson's plan was transformative. Johnson hired a team of outsiders to fill critical leadership positions, terminated more than 19,000 employees, ended the use of discounts, and ordered stores to be revamped without testing or validating whether any of his ideas would resonate with customers."

Sixteen months later, after initially being hailed as the savior of the company, Johnson was fired. In 2012, at the end of his

---

11. Also stated by Freddie Mercury when arguing with fictional record executive Ray Foster in the movie *Bohemian Rhapsody*.

first year as CEO, same-store sales fell 25 percent, the company recorded a $1 billion loss, and its stock fell 19.72 percent.[12] Customers abandoned JCPenney in droves. Johnson's vision had driven away the company's core customers *and* failed to attract new ones. When asked about the primary lesson Johnson learned from his tenure there, he stated he was a terrible fit for the organization.

The issue was his belief that his experiences at Apple and Target would transpose onto JCPenney. Johnson had extensive retail experience, handpicked his team, had support from the board of directors, and created the strategy himself. Yet Johnson's real failure was not having an intimate understanding of JCPenney customers.

Understanding the interests, preferences, and needs of customers isn't as easy as applying a previously successful formula. It's not just about identifying what to do, but also how to do it. Johnson's mindset on customer preferences was skewed by his past experiences. He succumbed to self-confirmation bias, using customer data that supported his existing beliefs to craft his strategy.

Loyal customers did voice their feedback, commenting, "He took away the feeling of small achievements when he got rid of coupons." Another noted, "You could buy big and tall clothes in a [JCPenney] store, not a catalog. They had that market cornered. Eliminating that is like the CEO just saying, 'too bad customer, go find it somewhere else.'" One other said, "Boutiques, juice bars with smoothies and coffee—no long-term customer of JCPenney cares about all that crap. They got away from what they did best."

JCPenney customers weren't looking for an experience; they were looking for deals. They were looking for hard-to-find specialty sizes. They enjoyed the unpretentious environment of a low-cost retailer that had an array of house brands with a high-quality reputation. Existing customers didn't want changes that would disrupt the core of what JCPenney stood for—value.

---

12. That's just in one day, on May 16, 2012.

Apple's word-of-mouth marketing and unique products drove customers to its stores. Apple didn't need conventional sales promotions to generate traffic. JCPenney didn't have a word-of-mouth machine, and its products weren't unique either. But JCPenney customers weren't getting bombarded with sales promotions when Ron Johnson did away with them by introducing an everyday low price and eliminating store coupons.

The challenge of catapulting JCPenney out of its slump required an intimate understanding of what was drawing customers to the business, what was making them stay, and conversely, what was driving others to the competition. Johnson didn't focus on finding problems or framing problems. He jumped to a familiar solution, one that wasn't grounded in rich customer intelligence and insights.

Context and Mindset

The JCPenney story isn't unusual. Many organizations work instinctually. We laud organizations like Apple and Tesla for their bold, non-customer-research-driven innovations. Elon Musk even said at a US Air Force tech conference, two weeks before the Tesla Cybertruck unveiling, that he does "zero market research whatsoever."

Musk's argument for ignoring customers isn't that they're wrong. Instead, he believes *he's* right. Musk also said at the conference, "A lot of times people try to make products they think others would love but they don't love themselves." Musk continued, "I find if you do [create products you love], people will want to buy it. If it's compelling to you it will be compelling to others." Even though Ron Johnson likely had this same passion and enthusiasm for his strategy, the context was completely different.

For Tesla, a brand-new, never-before-seen product (like the Cybertruck) is hard to truly visualize. An artificial focus group's input on a conceptual model would have been overly critical or overly complimentary. Musk knew customers would react very differently when a space-age-looking truck was rolled out with lasers and smoke. While experts can know customer needs better than customers themselves can, this insight is best applied to products that are revolutionary in nature.

Procter & Gamble did it this way with the original Swiffer, a dry-cloth alternative to a broom. There were a lot of expert R&D people working on the product who had developed their gut instincts for identifying big ideas. But their instincts were fostered through extensive immersion with customers, both through research, firsthand interactions, and conversations in context (such as observing and engaging people in real-world cleaning environments). Their experience coupled with insight enabled them to effectively think through layers of abstraction and get to a very unique solution.

At Apple, Johnson had innovative products that he could architect an experience around. At JCPenney, his mindset didn't translate. Johnson's strategy left the company in a worse condition than he found it.

Reframing Mindsets

Just as Johnson needed to shift his mindset, you also may need to reframe your thinking when identifying solutions to customer needs. Consider this: you are an office building manager, and your tenants are complaining about the elevator. It's old, slow, and they wait a long time for it to arrive. When you ask them for solutions, they have multiple suggestions: replace the elevator, install a new motor, or upgrade the software. These ideas share assumptions about what the problem is—the elevator is slow. Yet this is only one mindset.

The property owner takes another perspective, determining a much more elegant and cost-effective solution—put up mirrors by the elevator. This simple fix eliminated complaints because people lost track of time when given something to do (e.g., use the mirror to touch up their hair) other than watch the floor indicator. Other inexpensive distractions like this could include interesting signage or televisions streaming entertainment, news, or information.

This solution isn't the answer to the *tenant-stated* problem. It doesn't make the elevator faster. But it does solve the issue, albeit differently. Even though a new motor would have done the job, seeing the problem differently (reducing the *perceived* wait time versus the actual wait time) opened opportunities to discover alternative solutions.

Most customer problems and needs are multifaceted and can be addressed in multiple ways. For example, in 2012, Ryan O'Neill, head of customer experience for the travel website Expedia, had been sifting through data from the company's call center. He discovered for every one hundred people who booked travel on Expedia (reserving flights, hotels, or rental cars), fifty-eight of them placed a call for help.

Although customer service representatives were trained to make customers happy as quickly as possible, and short calls minimized expenses, O'Neill saw a flaw with this mindset. "The lens we were using was cost," said O'Neill. "We had always been focused on trying to reduce that cost. Instead of a ten-minute call, could we make it a two-minute call? But the real question was: Why any minutes?"

He discovered the number one reason customers called was to get a copy of their itinerary. In 2012, twenty million calls were logged for that purpose. It's akin to everyone in New York State calling Expedia in one year. At a cost of $5 per call, it was a $100 million problem.

Why weren't customers receiving their itineraries already? A myriad of small reasons. They mistyped their email address. Or the itinerary ended up in their spam folder. Or they deleted it by accident. And when customers did experience an itinerary delivery issue, there was no way to retrieve an itinerary from the company website.

Eliminating the mindset of reducing call time, Expedia focused on avoiding calls altogether by providing itinerary lookups online, saving millions of dollars in the process. While our past experiences and knowledge can be useful, they can cause us to fixate on an inefficient solution rather than reframing the problem to discover a new approach.

We all want to be confident in our own knowledge, experience, and expertise. Without it, what value would we bring to an organization? Yet everything we deliver in know-how can become inconsequential if we don't also apply an open mindset. One that is perpetually curious, continually exploring new perspectives, and constantly absorbing new information. What separates good from great is a fervor for discovery and, more importantly, questioning entrenched logic.

If you take nothing else from this chapter, remember that innovation can't manifest without an open mindset. As Voltaire said, "No problem can withstand the assault of sustained thinking."

5

Customer Centricity vs. Customer Ownership

Customer service shouldn't be a department; it should be the entire company.

—Tony Hsieh

A recent study from the CMO Council found only 11 percent of organizations believe their customers would characterize them as customer centric. Thousands of companies have been striving to become more customer focused for the past twenty years, so why have so few achieved it?

I spoke with a chief executive officer at a leading financial institution who defined customer centricity as "putting the customer at the heart of everything we do." What does that mean, *exactly*? They had no answer.

When it comes to translating a concept into action, you need specificity. If you have no definition of what customer centricity is, you could argue any initiative supports it. In addition, there is no measure for how effectively you put the customer at the heart of everything you do. Most companies point to net promoter scores[1] as the solution, but NPS only measures customer perceptions, not how customer centric the organization is.

> **What to think about through this chapter:**
> - Defining what customer centricity means to your organization
> - Understanding the impact of your company's structure on customers
> - How your organizational principles are impacting employee behaviors

The Downsides of Customer Centricity

The reality is not every customer wants to be at the heart of what every company does. You don't care whether the electric company puts you at the heart of their company. You just want a consistent, stable flow of electricity to your home at a fair price. You want a prompt response if there's a service disruption.

Consider how attempts at proactiveness can be viewed as intrusive, and attempts at customer centricity can be both inaccurate and irrelevant. Junk mail, spam, and online advertisements that follow you wherever you go—all frequently justified as customer centricity—are more like stalking than the behavior of a company that truly puts customer needs first.

However, the concept of customer centricity bodes well with the outward-facing parts of organizations, including marketing, sales, and service. For other departments, it can come off as a self-driven interest—a bit like "my area is most important."

---

1. You know how much I love these.

Imagine you are on the accounts receivable team, and you have a customer who is ninety days in arrears. How should you put the customer at the heart of what you do next? Allow them not to pay? Give them more time? It depends on how you characterize customer centricity. Arguably, it means different things to different companies as well as different departments within the same organization.

Customer Un-Centric

While many organizations strive to be more customer centric, others actually pursue the opposite. One company well known for its customer un-centricity is discount airline Ryanair. Ryanair is a low-budget airline headquartered in Dublin. Tickets are cheap and everything else (e.g., extra luggage or a specific seat on the plane) you pay extra for.

The company makes a profit any other airline would envy. Plus, the number of passengers who choose to fly with Ryanair continues to rise. In 2020, profits grew 13 percent and flight traffic grew to over 149 million flyers despite rising fuel prices on top of a global pandemic. A survey of twenty thousand Ryanair customers in 2018 found 92 percent said they would fly Ryanair again, with 87 percent stating they would recommend Ryanair to others and were satisfied with their experience.

Frans Reichardt, a customer-experience expert who's worked with companies including Phillips, Roche, and ING, sums up the airline's success perfectly in his blog, *The Customer Listener.* He writes, "Ryanair's success can be explained by the strategic choice of their main customer promise: a competitive price. The customer knows what to expect from Ryanair and, just as importantly, what not to. This works. Ryanair may not be particularly kind to their customers. Ryanair may not pamper them. Ryanair may not surprise them with free extras. Ryanair may deliver poor customer service. Ryanair excels in clarity at only one point: price." Many customers see this value and appreciate it. Being more customer centric in the traditional sense isn't necessary. In this circumstance, price *is* customer centricity.

Therefore, is customer centricity about making decisions that benefit your customers, potentially at the expense of your company's short-term profitability? Or is it serving customers only in the most efficient and cost-effective way for your business? Instead of focusing on the principle of customer centricity, companies should focus on the desired outcome—delivering value for customers in a way that differentiates them from the competition.

Who Owns the Customer?

If we agree the goal of customer centricity is to generate value for both customers and the company, how do we make sure what we do fits the bill?

The role of chief customer officer (CCO) was born to address this question. It was designed to ensure someone at an executive level was responsible for the total customer relationship. In a 2019 study, Gartner revealed that approximately 90 percent of organizations have a chief customer officer, chief experience officer, or equivalent role.

It's arguable, however, that everyone in a company shares responsibility for the customer relationship and that no single individual can own it. But without ownership, there's no accountability. So companies turn to a customer experience leader to fix issues that are creating unhappy customers.[2]

But when a senior Amazon executive was asked who owns the customer relationship, she was perplexed by the question. She responded, "Literally every single employee owns it." From her

---

2. Translated, this really means accelerating growth and revenue.

perspective, the idea of a single person or a small group responsible for the entire experience of millions of customers was completely ridiculous and utterly impossible. This is from a company whose core principles include being customer obsessed.[3]

It's much easier to assign responsibility to an individual rather than shape and educate an entire organization on how to influence the customer experience. Instead, they can aggregate information and feedback across the organization. They can be the single point of contact for insight and serve as a signal to the company that a customer focus is important. But prior to this role, did the function not exist? Was the customer completely ignored? Of course not. Every company, in some way, shape, or form understands its customers.

Historically, the capture, collection, and cataloging of customer information was the responsibility of sales and marketing. With the virtual speed-of-light expansion of digital commerce and hundreds of social media marketing platforms, traditional sales and marketing teams have become overwhelmed. The ability to conduct the activities which drive top-line growth, all while doing the detailed customer research, data gathering, and analysis is, for most companies, implausible. The slow-moving, deep-dive examination gets pushed to the back burner and replaced with broad generalizations and immediately actionable initiatives. The holistic view and understanding of the customer experience is lost, and so the chief customer officer neatly fills the void.

Appointing someone to this role, however, is often a cursory attempt to disguise the true, non-customer-focused nature of the organization. Given a team of resources, a chief customer officer may, in theory, be able to aggregate siloed customer data and identify strategic areas for change. In reality, if the organization as a

---

3. Aside from whether you love them, hate them, or disagree with some of their policies.

whole isn't driven to continually examine how to better serve and engage customers, any change endeavor will be futile.

If a department's performance is measured on accomplishing specific initiatives, the chief customer officer strolling in with a new customer project may come off as an unwelcome distraction. If the organization is fully versed on how to understand, analyze, and capitalize on customer data and insights, they can identify and act on problems and opportunities independently, without a directive from a CCO.

While there's a time and place for a CCO, it takes eyes and abilities across the entire organization to bring any customer focus to life. If customer centricity is your organizational purpose, then it takes the entire organization. A CCO can't be a surrogate.

At the Heart of Everything We Do

This returns us to the definition of putting the customer at the heart of everything we do. A truly customer-centric organization gives every functional area access to customer input. But with unvarnished feedback, tough questions arise. Can we afford to do what customers are asking for? How do we choose between conflicting needs? If you're not examining candid customer insights, you'll never be faced with these challenges, but you also won't truly understand your customers.

Rick Rubin, American record producer and former copresident of Columbia Records, said it best: "If you only know your customers through their transactional data . . . if you only speak to your customers to hear what they think about you, rather than understand what you don't know about them . . . if you only talk about your customers in generic terms . . . if you think your customers only care about you and what you do . . . if you think your customers' lives have remained the same for over a year . . . if you use trend reports as a substitute for knowing your customers' future habits and behaviors . . . if you only talk to the same customers in the same markets . . . if you only care about how to get your customers to buy more of what you're selling . . . if you call your customers 'purchasers' . . . then I assure you, you don't know or truly care about your customers."

He's not wrong. Caring requires knowing. Knowing requires understanding people as individuals, not simply as a revenue source. Achieving this means shrinking the gap between you and your customers. And getting as close as possible requires an organizational structure that enables doing so.

Structure, Communication, and Behavior

Your organizational structure is your operational construct. It determines how activities and information flow throughout the business. It also drives and supports organizational behaviors.

For example, if you provide customers the lowest prices, is *everyone* in the organization focused on cost control? If your brand is built on amazing service, does *everyone*[4] clearly understand how they can influence the service experience? What behaviors are nonnegotiable, and how do you ensure you're enabling, eliminating, or reinforcing them? W. Edward Deming, engineer and quality management thinker, said, "A bad system will beat a good person every time." In short, a poor structure can hamper customer centricity if the right behaviors aren't reinforcing it.

Most companies have some form of a traditional, hierarchical organization for good reason. As noted by Peter Drucker in 1999, "There has to be a final authority, someone who can make the final decision and [own it]." Yet organizational structures tend to evolve haphazardly over time, driven by internal politics rather than

---

4. Not just sales or customer service, but even back-office functions like accounting and procurement.

strategic customer objectives. This results in turf wars, which kill collaboration and knowledge sharing, signal the death of promising opportunities due to leadership inattention, and stall initiatives because priorities are fragmented or unfocused.

To fix these issues, companies often create complementary overlays to work within the existing hierarchy. This typically takes the form of project teams, committees, or specialized departments, each with more community-like features. But these tangential groups are usually considered less important and are often isolated from the main hierarchy, creating even more organizational fragmentation.

Structures Need Frameworks

Every organizational structure encompasses numerous components, including departments, roles, responsibilities, reporting channels, workflows, and so on. These are essential operating mechanisms in any organization, whether customer centric or not. However, improving your customer focus isn't simply a matter of altering structures and processes, but changing behaviors—what people do and how they act, interact, communicate, and make judgments and decisions. Identifying and examining current employee behaviors, defining desired behaviors, and generating new, relevant ones requires a framework, a set of actionable principles that guide behaviors and actions which are both modeled and encouraged.

These principles should specify both the how (e.g., how we do things, how we treat others, and so on) and the what (e.g., what we say, what we do, and the like). But these principles aren't simply a list of cliché organizational values or a generic mission statement. They give specificity to your objectives. For example, if an organizational objective includes putting customers first, behavioral principles explain what specific behaviors represent that objective, ways to articulate it to others, and how to put it into action.

Clear principles create a shared understanding and a common vocabulary, enabling everyone in the organization to improve communication, unity, and alignment, along with diminishing layers, reducing handoffs, and shrinking communication lines. A 2011 Bain and Company study of two hundred organizations revealed that 83 percent of the best-performing businesses had established explicit, widely understood, and easily applied customer-centric behavioral principles across their organizations.

Principles Support Behaviors

A great example of customer-centric behavioral principles applied organization-wide can be found in Olam International. Olam is a major food and agri-business company, operating in sixty countries, supplying food and raw materials to over 19,800 customers worldwide. The company manages customer-centric behavioral principles right from the farm gate. Olam requires managers to live in the rural areas of developing countries to learn what really goes on at farms. This nonnegotiable principle is the foundation for hiring requirements, individual assignments, and training content. In addition, each manager is to give the highest priority to their relationships with local farmers. Requirements for key behaviors and routines in support of this principle are outlined in detail throughout their field operating manual. The company's customer principles, and the practices which support them, are central to its operational success.

Keep in mind, organizational structures affect behaviors greatly because reporting relationships are the basis of power. A department manager has power over their subordinates by influencing things they have access to, including information, assignments, compensation, and career opportunities. If your company simply focuses on redesigning structures rather than shaping behaviors, the result is often added complexity and bureaucracy—further shrinking the customer focus. While we traditionally view organizational structure as the method to solve operational problems, principles and behaviors are what create customer centricity.

One way to begin shaping customer-focused behaviors is by changing the old methods of defining organizational purpose— those all-too-familiar vision, mission, and values statements. Rather than utilize these to define what your *company* wants, flip the perspective to what your *customer* wants, starting with your mission statement.

Kill Your Mission Statement

A traditional mission statement is mostly filled with vague and meaningless buzzwords. If your employees can't relate to your mission statement or articulate its essence, then it won't mean much to anyone else. Take the traditional mission statement from a major auto manufacturer:

> *By creating value for our customers, we create value for our shareholders. We use our expertise to create transport-related products and services of superior quality, safety, and environmental care for demanding customers in selected segments. We work with energy, passion, and respect for the individual.*

What is that generic garbage? Of course the organization is going to create value—everyone does in one way or another. Of course the company will use their expertise to create products of superior quality, because no one would say the opposite. Working with energy and passion? No shit! Why would we work *without* energy or passion?

The problem is, mission statements shouldn't start with your company, but with your customer. You need a customer mission. A customer mission resets the goalposts—helping shift the organizational mindset outward (to the customer) rather than inward (to the organization). It is as much what it's not about as what it is about.

What a customer mission isn't about:

1. It's not about you (*the company*).
2. It's not about how you do it (*the process*).
3. It's not about generic terminology (*the corporate speak*).

What a customer mission is about:

1. It is about who you serve (*the customers*).
2. It is about outcomes (*the results*).
3. It is about authentic expression (*the purpose*).

There are four distinct components to a well-crafted customer mission:

1. Instead of "what we do," articulate "*what our customers want to accomplish/achieve.*"
2. Instead of "how we do it," articulate "*how our customers want to be served.*"
3. Instead of saying "what value we bring," describe "*the impact we have on our customers.*"
4. Instead of "why we do it," explain "*why our customers care about what we do.*"

Consider Fastenal, an American industrial supply company based in Winona, Minnesota, that as of 2018 had over 2,600 branches across the United States, Canada, Mexico, and Europe. Here's their traditional mission statement:

Our mission is to grow our company by providing our customers with a superior offering of products, consumption tracking capabilities and Reseller Consortium partners. We recognize that supplier diversity is an opportunity for Fastenal to establish a competitive advantage and improve customer satisfaction.

While their motto is "Growth through customer service," their mission statement says very little about "how" and "why" from a customer perspective. A customer mission statement for Fastenal would be designed more like the following:

PURPOSE: "Our purpose is to provide customers with tools and equipment that are right for the job, right when they need it."
HOW: "We provide this by consistently expanding offerings through both digital and physical channels, improving the efficiency and effectiveness of the job customers want accomplished."
OUTCOME: "Our goal is to continually find and deliver new ways to help our customers deliver on *their* promises."

As this example shows, the shift toward a customer-focused mentality transforms the traditional mission statement into something much clearer and more actionable for employees. It provides a direction and purpose. So throw out your old mission statement. It's probably something you don't use anyway.

If you take nothing else from this chapter, remember customer centricity is about behaviors. Behaviors can't change without a clear definition of what is acceptable, what is not, and why. And if everyone in the organization isn't aligned with that why, they can't effectively translate it into action.

The Impact of
Company Culture

For organizations, culture is destiny.

—Tony Hsieh

Company culture is the *way* things get done in your organization on a day-to-day basis. It is a culmination of actions and intangibles (i.e., beliefs and attitudes) that characterize the company's practices and embody its principles. Well-functioning company cultures are both viscous and fluid, helping attract and retain great talent, while making it easy for that talent to implement the organization's business strategy.

A culture's effectiveness depends on whether it supports or hinders achieving that strategy. Of course, this doesn't mean there aren't cultures we dislike or even despise. But likability doesn't equate to effectiveness. An unappealing organizational culture may be perfectly aligned with a specific business strategy and effectively supports its implementation.

> ## What to think about through this chapter:
>
> - Whether your company culture is connected to customers
> - Why customer centricity requires getting all employees involved
> - How to unite customer data, company culture, and organizational strategy

Which Way Does Your Culture Face?

Multiple studies have shown that customer-centric organizations are over 60 percent more profitable year-over-year than those who prioritize internal metrics and objectives. However, this isn't accomplished only by changing culture—it first requires a shift in strategy and organizational priorities.

Jack Welch, former chief of General Electric, stated, "An organization with its face toward the CEO has its ass toward the customer." Essentially, when it comes to your strategic focus, there's only one direction you can face at a time—inward or outward. This means organizations need explicit priorities that work together harmoniously. Many companies hold conflicting strategic priorities, which creates cultural misalignment. We're customer focused, but highly cost controlling. We're all about innovation, but completely metrics driven. We're risk-takers but want proof before we invest.

Many CEOs would say their companies don't have the luxury to choose between facing inward and outward. They must spend money to grow and retain customers, but also reduce internal costs and minimize risks. Yet an organization's true priorities are reflected in its behaviors.[1] A CEO may proclaim the organization's

---

1. A familiar refrain from the previous chapter.

priority is innovation, but if the company culture is focused and rewarded on operational efficiency, employees aren't going to waste time on idea exploration and experimental trial and error. In short, the cultural-strategic misalignment hinders the company's ability to behave in a way that drives customer innovation.

The Story of Trader Joe's

Trader Joe's is well known for being a highly customer-centric organization. The US grocer has built a cultlike following over the years. They also enjoy the industry's highest sales—$1,734 per square foot. (In comparison, Whole Foods only sells $930 per square foot.) They make an intentional effort to get closer to their customers, to see and solve their problems. Employees regularly interact with customers directly to get their input and feedback. Even the CEO, Dan Bane, often works in the stores as a bagger, capturing customer insights.

He recently told the story of one memorable customer interaction. "We used to sell bananas by the pound, like everybody else, but because we don't have scales in the store, we had to weigh them and package them in little plastic bags in the warehouse before they got shipped out . . . usually the smallest bag you could buy, was like four or five bananas. A customer . . . nice little lady . . . comes up and looks at all the packages [of bananas] but didn't put one in her cart. And so, I asked her, 'Ma'am, if you don't mind me asking, I saw you looking at the bananas, but you didn't, you didn't put anything in your cart.' And she says to me, 'Sonny, I may not live to that fourth banana.' And so, we decided the next day we were going to sell individual bananas. And they've been nineteen cents ever since."

At Trader Joe's, receiving customer feedback is not about driving concerns to a call center filled with trained, friendly service representatives. Rather, they believe in direct human interaction— between customers, captains, and crew members (as their managers and employees are called). "It's best for us to get out into the world and not just wait for things to come to us," Bane notes.

Trader Joe's doesn't use analytics, customer relationship management systems, or any other special methods to target, segment, or track its customers. Instead, the organization relies on its people to facilitate a unique customer intimacy, enabling the delivery of experiences customers want. This means impersonal Big Data isn't a part of the organizational strategy. Matt Sloan, vice president of marketing, noted, "We don't have access to your data at Trader Joe's because we don't have any data on you."

A key component to Trader Joe's strategy is the company considers each store its own business. It empowers each store to do what fits its neighborhood and customer base. Managers (captains) are responsible for identifying how to improve and grow their store's business. Trader Joe's in Reno, Nevada, was able to locally stock a customer's request for her favorite soy ice cream cookie after having tasted it at a Southern California location. The Phoenix, Arizona, Trader Joe's started opening well before their official open at 9:00 a.m., just so customers could shop at the most convenient time for them.

Trader Joe's doesn't sell online or wholesale, even though doing so could help speed more profitable growth. "Our products work the best when they're sold as part of this overall customer experience within the store," Bane says. "We're not ready to give that up. For us, the brand is too important, and the store is our brand."

In short, the organization could grow faster, but they consciously and strategically choose not to. When asked to speak on the company's future growth, Bane said, "We're targeting to open thirty to thirty-five stores a year in the forty-eight states . . . the only thing that holds us back is having the right number of captains and crew members to open up great stores. So we won't open a store just because we can, we want to open a store that's run by the right kind of people doing the right kinds of things, and that's really important to us."

What Sets Trader Joe's Apart

Trader Joe's continually works to improve the customer experience. They don't just want to capture customer feedback, but also effectively respond to it. Captains spend most of their days on the retail floor, directly interacting with customers and immediately altering the store and its products to address those needs. Crew members, when asked about a product, respond instantly by bringing it to the customer, opening it, and indulging in a taste test with them to get their opinion. Trader Joe's also refunds the money for any product a customer is not satisfied with despite having been opened and consumed.

Crew members also have the autonomy to make and act on bigger decisions in a customer's best interest. An eighty-nine-year-old man was snowed in at his Pennsylvanian home around the holidays and, after calling multiple grocers, couldn't find anyone to deliver. However, his local Trader Joe's, which usually does not deliver, chose to make an exception in his case. In addition, the food was delivered less than thirty minutes later, paid in full.[2]

Why We Do the Things We Do

While we might admire Trader Joe's success, it's critical to understand *how* they did it. Was it by having great policies and procedures? Or hiring and training the right employees? Or having innovative leadership in place? The answer goes back to culture-strategy

---

2. This was prior to DoorDash, Postmates, and other delivery services.

alignment and every person in the organization understanding why they do the things they do.

It could be said Trader Joe's advantage comes from low prices, cost controls, and superior private-label products, but these are only components of their bigger strategy—understanding their customers better than their competitors do. It is the differentiating purpose or their "why." It guides employee behaviors. It governs every organizational decision, from what products to stock to shaping in-store experiences. This purpose is the foundation for the entire Trader Joe's operation.

Without a distinct and differentiating purpose, priorities become a moving target. For example, you may emphasize going above and beyond to serve customers one day and turn around and cut customer support the next. Or preach the urgency of growing the customer base, while incentivizing sales teams to increase revenues from existing customers. Or lauding the importance of innovation and the creation of game-changing solutions, all the while refusing to fund or support research or pilot projects. When organizations attempt to be all things to all stakeholders, resources are inevitably pulled in divergent directions.

In a recent conversation with the CEO of a global manufacturer, they said this about their company's differentiating purpose: "Well, of course, it's providing our customers with the best quality products and the most responsive service. But we also must serve our shareholders, and sometimes they have different priorities we need to consider. We always need to keep in mind that we're in business to grow profitably." There's no question every company is in business to grow profitably.[3] But Trader Joe's didn't make being the most

---

3. Duh.

profitable grocer their highest priority; they tried to be the grocer most in tune with their customer, and the profits have followed.

The Culture-Strategy-Customer Relationship

Which comes first, culture or strategy? The common belief is that putting culture first will cause customer centricity to follow. This often leads to an emphasis on increasing employee happiness and satisfaction—providing free food, game rooms, after-work parties, and transformed workspaces. However, these things don't contribute directly to improving customer-focused behaviors.

We know that when employees are engaged, they put more time and effort into serving customer needs. Multiple Gallup studies report the most engaged organizations on average experience 22 percent higher productivity and profitability than their competitors. Organizations that *help* employees put *customers* first—with the right tools, resources, skills, support, and training—have more sustainable results. If the organization doesn't use customer needs and insights to shape its strategy, culture, and business model, implementing an employee-first culture risks becoming internally focused and externally irrelevant.

A national industrial insurer struggled with this balance. In 2019, they identified one of the major risks to organizational growth was their aging workforce. Though they began an aggressive recruitment campaign for new talent, younger hires would stay at the company on average for eighteen months and refer to the company culture in exit interviews as stagnant, dated, and rigid. There was a need for change.

The leadership team conducted an in-depth study, examining organizational culture and identifying areas of weakness. The goal was to reshape the culture around customer centricity and open communication. The team created a new set of organizational values, modernized the mission statement, and held a series of employee feedback forums and town halls to shape internal messaging. It was a solid strategy, in theory.

The reality was the organization's *actual* strategy and key performance metrics were all financially driven. This led to a strong focus on keeping costs low and minimizing risks. While the leadership team was attempting to transform culture, they failed to address this misalignment.

For example, the new cultural values emphasized customer responsiveness, but the organization's technological infrastructure was incredibly outdated and required manual, redundant workarounds. Customers were making constant requests to pay invoices online, but their only option was to mail a check, which was not only inconvenient for customers, but also consumed extensive internal time and resources to process.

Open communication initiatives meant to encourage employees to speak up about ways to change the company for the better were met with resistance, citing the company's focus on reducing expenses. When a department spoke up about a demeaning and aggressive manager, leadership skirted the request, citing the manager's impending retirement date two years away. A new hire took the initiative to advance their Microsoft Excel skills, only to learn the company's version was three years old, and she couldn't apply what she learned from the up-to-date classroom version.

Fundamental Disconnect

Culture, customer orientation, and organizational strategy are a triumvirate—all three hold equal power. Making a concerted effort to change one aspect while ignoring or short-changing the other two threatens to derail your work. The disconnect between all three areas was the industrial insurer's major obstacle to organizational growth. No matter how encouraged they were to deliver stellar service to customers, employees' hands were tied when it came to serving them more efficiently and proactively. Culture change itself couldn't overcome the lack of a clear customer-centric strategy and structure. Since they all intersect, they can't be tackled independently—just like an employee can't truly be happy without the tools and infrastructure to do their job well.[4]

Connecting Customers with Culture

Many organizations strive to create a healthy culture, where employees are trained, respected, trusted, and rewarded for behaviors that reflect the organization's principles. However, training and respect isn't enough to close the gap between employees and customers. Employees need the freedom to interact and engage with customers to gain a more intimate understanding of their needs.

But as organizations grow, this freedom is curtailed. Discovery and exploration are replaced with processes and hierarchy to address the chaos and complexity of a large organization with a lot of moving parts. This layered bureaucracy builds in structured stability designed to minimize mistakes. Yet this structure minimizes critical thinking and, over time, diminishes the organization's creative abilities. These rigid processes also hinder quick adaptation and responsiveness to changing customer needs, as employees become focused on following process and adhering to a system.

So the tug-of-war begins. Companies seek new innovations and insights, and must attempt to insert intuition and nuance in an operational structure designed to eliminate it. One way to counter this is by charging all employees to gather customer insights regularly.

---

4. If you take nothing else from this book, don't forget this part.

Making Feedback Capture Everyone's Job

How do you make capturing feedback everyone's job? It requires making customer engagement the first priority. It requires creating time and opportunity for every employee to capture input. It requires making it a part of the job description. Alessandro Di Fiore, in a 2019 article for *Harvard Business Review,* shared a case study of this concept in action.

His article highlighted Arena swimwear, which uses its sales representatives in the field to capture customer insights. Those field representatives discovered that beginner swimmers often went to the pool only a few times and then quit because they struggled to develop good breathing techniques. When these insights were brought back to the organization, Arena developed the Freestyle Breather, a pair of plastic foils that could be attached to a novice swimmer's goggles. The direct observations from the field led to a new solution to a hidden problem—why novice swimmers quit. This insight wouldn't have been uncovered without direct exposure to the customer's environment.

Insights can also be captured from those who don't usually interact with customers, like finance or administrative teams. Intuit embedded the practice of customer exploration into the job descriptions of all employees, requiring them to spend a minimum of three hours per month with customers.

At Davide Oldani's Michelin-starred restaurant D'O in Milan, there are no waiters. The chefs take food orders from customers, enabling them to experience their needs in the context of the restaurant, providing them the ability to better understand customers' evolving needs.

When you expand customer exploration across the organization, an exponential number of insights can be captured, without disruption or significant costs. One of our clients has 480 employees. If each of them spends two hours per month engaging with customers, 960 hours of customer research is captured, equivalent to

11,520 hours a year. The cost of that type of research using a third party would be ungodly. Capturing this amount of insight enables the organization to uncover revolutionary ideas, all the while letting employees expand their skills, gain a better understanding of customers, and increase the value they deliver to the company.

If you take nothing else from this chapter, remember organizational strategy, culture, and customer focus must all align. Otherwise, you'll end up playing organizational "whac-a-mole," reacting to the next misalignment as it pops up—frequently, in perpetuity.

7

Customer Action Learning

Opportunities multiply as they are seized.

—Sun Tzu

The urgency of getting things done unfailingly hijacks the luxury of learning. With constant pressures to meet goals and show progress, organizations try to keep their proverbial machines humming by maintaining a quick pace of activities and decision-making. Employees, and even organizations themselves, end up short-changed by this emphasis on productivity because innovations aren't born from constant distractions.

Learning about customer needs and generating innovative ideas requires time and opportunity. Time to capture detailed feedback and reflect on observations. Time to have immersive conversations with others, where collaboration and productive dialogue can occur. Opportunity for exposure to different perspectives, people, and situations. Yet how many employees have the bandwidth, energy, and enthusiasm to do this? Not enough.

> ## What to think about through this chapter:
> - Why we (all) need time to reflect
> - Why learning by doing is essential
> - How jumping to solutions kills innovation

Wasted Time

It's clear that excess bureaucracy, antiquated policies and procedures, and unproductive meetings can be massive time sucks. While it's debatable how much time is truly wasted inside organizations,[1] the more revealing question is how we're defining *wasted time*.

The most cited study on wasted time, conducted by Salary.com in 2014, asked 750 people to estimate how much of their time at work was unproductive and why. Even though they noted general distractions like social media, over 53 percent of respondents said they wasted time taking short breaks because they believed it increased their overall productivity. This albeit dated study indicates that, intuitively, people know they need to break up their days to spend time on mental processing.

As Albert Einstein said, "Education is not the learning of facts but teaching the mind to think." This teaching can't be accomplished in a single exercise, yet organizations continually try to formalize the process through workshops or seminars. This usually takes the form of quirky problem-solving activities, such as the marshmallow spaghetti tower[2] or the old-fashioned brainstorming session. Not surprisingly, these fail to change behaviors or sustainably generate transformative ideas.

---

1. Studies claim it ranges from thirty minutes to five hours daily per employee.

2. The marshmallow spaghetti tower is an exercise where a team is given spaghetti, tape, a string, and eighteen minutes to build the tallest possible tower that can support a marshmallow.

Back to Tech

Some organizations will try to use training software to help employees become better critical thinkers, idea generators, and problem solvers. This includes webinars, online courses, and pro- grams developed in-house. Regrettably, these are frequently out- dated and lack the multimodal education capabilities (reading, writing, visual, and kinesthetic) necessary for deeper learning. In addition, there's rarely a plan in place to translate the training into action on the job. In the end, learning ends up getting relegated to being an important-but-never-urgent initiative.

Learning in this proverbial bubble is akin to being given one private tennis lesson and then walking into a national competi- tion. The best tennis coach can't make someone a better player if that individual doesn't practice and continually refine their game. You'll also never build a great group of tennis players if only a couple of players are receiving ongoing lessons. Learning must be a behavior and routine, not relegated to a select few or isolated to select periods throughout the year. It must be integrated into employees' daily working lives.

Defining Action Learning

This is where action learning, or learning by doing, comes in. The concept was conceived in the early 1980s by the late Reg Revans, a management professor and consultant. From his time at Cam- bridge, Revans remembered Albert Einstein[3] saying to him, "If you think you understand a problem, make sure you are not deceiving yourself." This helped Revans see the key to improving problem- solving wasn't with experts, but with nonexperts, drawing a delineation between knowledge and wisdom. He developed a pro- cess where individuals would work and learn simultaneously, by

---

3. Isn't he the best?

tackling real issues with real consequences. Action learning is meant to foster independent, critical, and creative thinking through a process of insightful questioning and reflective listening.

Confucius[4] once said, "I hear, and I forget; I see, and I remember; I do, and I understand." His belief was that one should engage in a process of deliberation in advance of taking action. By having small groups collaboratively tackling *actual* organizational challenges, defining root problems, identifying possible solutions, acting on them, and discussing outcomes, individuals become exposed to different perspectives, ideas, and new ways of thinking.

Here's how it fundamentally works: A group of people are divided into teams and tasked with solving the same organizational problem. Each team defines the nature of the problem and determines the approaches they would take to resolve it. The teams then present their approaches, while the other teams ask probing questions on what they see, hear, and feel. As participants listen to the presentations and dialogue, they are exposed to the different ways in which the problem could be framed and solved. In a customer context, action learning centers on defining, evaluating, analyzing, discussing, and crafting a solution to a customer problem. This includes participants getting hands-on with customers, questioning assumptions, researching insights, and collaborating with others. For employees accustomed to passively engaging, listening, and note taking, this approach can be difficult. On the other hand, many enjoy the opportunity and rise to the challenge.

Action Learning in Action

Selecting the right problem to tackle with action learning is important. Boeing's Global Leadership Action Learning Program

---

4. He's pretty cool too.

selects real business issues and problems that are critical to resolve and require prompt attention. But action learning doesn't apply exclusively to tackling business or customer problems. Novartis, a world leader in health care, formed action learning groups with six noncompetitive organizations to work on shared issues, including marketing strategies, that cut across all their companies.

Another key use of action learning is to develop leadership skills and strengthen business acumen. At Boeing, their action learning program is targeted at developing executive skills in adapting, thinking globally, building relationships, inspiring trust, leading courageously, influencing, and negotiating. Siemens uses action learning to help the company maximize entrepreneurial spirit, enhance cooperation, and increase the free exchange of ideas. Corning Inc. uses action learning for diversity training, in which gender- and race-balanced groups work through issues involving sexual and racial bias.

There is also widespread use of action learning in universities and public schools. The McGill University MBA program in Canada and the University of Michigan MBA program are based on the principles of action learning. The principals and assistant principals of Fairfax County Public Schools in Virginia have used action learning teams to explore and develop strategies for numerous communication challenges, including how to deal with angry, demanding parents, and how to handle and supervise ineffective teachers.

Solution Jumping

One of the biggest impediments to action learning is solution jumping. The combination of time pressures and lack of creative problem-solving skills frequently lead individuals and teams to quickly define the customer problem—without seeking additional perspectives—and identify an immediate solution. Solution jumping is dangerous. Not only does it frequently fail to address the root of a problem, but it also feeds and amplifies our cognitive biases.[5]

The initial definition of a problem is often our own perception of it. What we see on the surface is filtered through our own experiences, knowledge, and backgrounds. However, problems are often complex. By jumping to a solution, we overlook the myriad alternative ways it can be tackled, simply for the sake of perceived progress. Creative and innovative solutions always come from better clarification of a problem.

To best clarify a problem, it needs to be seen firsthand. One way to do this using lean methodologies[6] is called a Gemba Walk,[7] where employees conduct in-person, on-location observation of a process, and interact with the employees conducting it, asking questions, and learning directly. The goal is not to point out on-the-spot fixes, but to listen to suggestions, complaints, and comments, and then to later reflect on the best approach for making improvements.

Gemba Walk principles can be applied to customers as well, through direct engagement and observation in their own environments. For example, say a customer was sharing their experience working with a specific accounting software. From an initial survey, they had noted their satisfaction and shared no suggestions on how to improve the platform. Yet when observed using the software in context, the customer applied a series of unconscious workarounds, including Post-it notes and spreadsheets, which weren't mentioned in the survey. The customer didn't consider the

---

5. Refer to earlier chapters for a refresher on biases and heuristics.

6. A way of optimizing the people, resources, effort, and energy of your organization toward creating value for the customer.

7. The Gemba Walk is an observational tool providing individuals the opportunity to stand back from their day-to-day tasks and walk the floor of their workplace to identify wasteful activities. The original Japanese term is *Genchi Genbutsu*, which means "real thing" or "real place."

workarounds as problems because they were simply used to them. Without seeing these actions firsthand, there would be no opportunity to explore how they could be addressed or eliminated.

Why Not Use Big Data Instead?

Big Data has its limits when it comes to learning about customers. After all, data only exists about the past, it can't answer a question you didn't think to ask, and it can't reveal what customers can't easily articulate.

Big Data is also precisely inaccurate.[8] A 2017 Deloitte third-party data study revealed 75 percent of respondents said their data was 0 to 50 percent correct. One third said the information was less than 25 percent correct. While engaging with customers may not be as exciting as investing in Big Data, it consistently generates accurate insights.

When Toyota planned to design a luxury car for the United States, they didn't sift through survey data from existing Toyota customers about current Toyota models. Instead, they sent designers to California, where they could directly observe and interview target customers to learn what they were seeking in a car. This intimate knowledge resulted in a completely new luxury car brand—better known today as Lexus. Listening to and engaging with customers is now an integral part of Toyota's organizational behavior. Instead of relying on Big Data for customer insights, go out and talk to people. While Big Data is great, it's no substitute for direct observation and one-on-one conversation.

We can't effectively learn without taking the time to do so. We teach our children effectively not by showing them a PowerPoint or having them watch a training video, but enabling them to be

---

8. Again, it has its place in certain circumstances.

hands-on, practice things repeatedly, and become immersed in situations that foster understanding. We remind them often where there are opportunities to expand their perspectives. We don't punish their first-time failures but capitalize on them as learning opportunities. Adults learn in the same way. If you take nothing else from this chapter, remember that to effectively learn about customers, you must get out of the office and into real customer environments.

8

Shifting Mindsets and Learning What to Ask

It is all about the survival of the fastest.
—Jeremy Waite

It's easy to say we should capture more explicit customer feedback. It's much harder to actually do, so organizations find reasons to avoid it. In a 2019 qualitative survey of thirty midmarket companies, excuses for not getting customer feedback ran the gamut. They fell into four major categories: cost, effectiveness, execution, and brand/revenue impact.

- Customer contact data was unclean or inaccurate (ineffective)
- Takes too much time or resources (too costly)
- Previous attempts at feedback capture created little value (ineffective)
- Concerns about potentially low participation (ineffective)
- Concerns about how customers will perceive an interview or survey (impacts brand)

- Worried about it revealing needs they can't address (can't deliver)
- Worried about impacting relationship with a salesperson (impacts sales)
- Concerned about managing follow-up expectations (can't deliver)
- Can't conduct internally or don't have trained talent (can't deliver)
- Concerned about the price of outsourcing (too costly)
- Worried it will annoy customers (impacts brand)
- Concerned the organization won't be able to translate into action (can't deliver)

These concerns are not uncommon because past experiences can influence expectations and reinforce biases. Yet if there's an entrenched belief that deep customer understanding is irrelevant, efforts to discover insights will become clandestine or, even worse, dismissed when revealed.

What to think about through this chapter:

- Why customer interaction is critical to better customer knowledge
- How to get your organization's mindset into the customer's shoes using 3W
- Designing your customer Wow hypothesis and how to validate it

Surveys Pros and Cons

Surveys are our default go-to for capturing feedback, and they definitely have their place. For example, surveys are excellent for gathering high-level, overarching sentiments from customers, including brand perceptions or general satisfaction levels. In more targeted applications, surveys can capture statistically representative samples of opinions on specific products or service features. However, surveys can also be misleading. When architected poorly, built-in biases can arise, skewing responses and creating deceptive conclusions.

For instance, respondents can change their behaviors and opinions simply by taking part in a survey. Because people can often deduce the aim of a survey, they may answer in ways that support its objective rather than in ways that reveal what they truly think, resulting in deceiving responses. People may also overreport or underreport their viewpoints on questions that are socially polarizing or only have extreme answer choices (e.g., none, never, or always). In addition, they may simply respond in agreement to all the questions in a survey, making the information quite useless.

Survey responses can also be unintentionally interpreted as fact rather than simply an indicator of customer perceptions. Instead of utilizing the data as a starting point for further exploration, companies attempt to use it as a silver bullet to justify new features, services, or products rather than a starting point for identifying the need behind the need.

How a Conversation Changes Things

Direct customer interaction and engagement is different. Having a dialogue with an individual, in a context where you can observe them using a product or trying to solve a problem, reveals information that can't be captured through any survey. There's an opportunity to observe nuances, conduct deep questioning, and build rapport. Yet these insights can be abstract. They aren't as clear-cut as customer transactions or purchase trends.

When seeking novel ideas, structured data doesn't help in the way conversations and observations can. Data about an individual's actions may identify hiccups and roadblocks within a process but doesn't reveal what's causing those issues. For example, an application form with a high abandonment rate may indicate that people are having trouble completing the form, are asked for information they can't easily provide, or have other usability issues. It can't tell you how people are feeling, what they're thinking, or what other concerns may influence their behavior.

Ford Engaged

Ford Motor Company recently redesigned its iconic Bronco model. Even as a massive, one-hundred-year-old company with decades of customer research at hand, they didn't choose to use it. Instead, they went out and conducted thousands of hours of in-person discussions with real customers, getting to know real people. They spoke with people who lived in cities, people who heavily modify their vehicles, and those who aren't happy unless they are hanging off the side of a mountain.

In addition to seeking new customer knowledge, Ford also took a novel approach to the design process. Instead of beginning with traditional drawings, they conducted human-centered research. Their focus was on identifying specific problems, looking very deeply at customers, working out what was going on in their lives, and determining how they could make things easier, better, and more fulfilling. In short, a customer-first mentality led the project.

Their process included weekly customer-focused storytelling exercises that recapped and illustrated specific customer needs and scenarios. The team challenged themselves to look closer at what they were designing for—asking customers questions not just about utilization but also contextual factors, such as weather, temperature, ground conditions, if driving alone or with others, and more. This attention to customer detail has caused Ford to receive more than 125,000 orders for the Bronco to date, and 190,000 people having put down $100 refundable deposits. Ford has currently stopped taking reservations due to the overwhelming demand.

American Express Conversed

American Express saw similar success with the 2017 launch of their Pay-It Plan-It program. They conducted over 120 in-person interviews with Millennials to understand their payment behaviors around debt and credit, and their mindsets around borrowing and spending. One interviewee discussed their monthly panic when receiving their credit card statement, and their habit of making multiple payments over the course of the month to quell their anxiety of receiving a big end-of-month bill. Others were wary of credit cards due to past financial mistakes and avoided accruing balances to pay off.

In a highly regulated and complex industry, the challenge was finding a unique differentiator for credit card offerings outside of simply piling on more rewards. The team focused on one customer desire that consistently came up in their interviews—the need for flexibility and transparency when paying for big purchases. Customers viewed credit cards as a service, not as a product like the American Express team did. They also saw credit cards as a payment method rather than a loan, even though American Express saw themselves as a lender. This meant customers were not seeking another lending feature, but a new way to pay their bills—specifically, for those large purchases.

So the American Express team developed a new card feature that allowed customers to pay for purchases over $100 (such as an unexpected vet bill) by dividing them into equal payments with a fixed fee and no interest. They could choose from three monthly plan offerings, ranging from three to twenty-four months, so there would be no surprises. Paying early was also penalty free. Since launching the program in 2017, American Express customers have created nearly five million payment plans, totaling nearly $4 billion in purchases, with an average plan size of $789, and Millennials making up 44 percent of all plans.

How We're Told to Do It

While it might seem Ford and American Express captured some magic that eludes the average organization, this isn't the case. Capturing and dissecting customer insights is a learned skill, not a fixed rubric. It's not developed overnight. Just like becoming a concert violinist, it requires considerable amounts of practice and refinement.

Entrepreneurship program curriculums instruct start-ups to create hypotheses and test them against customer feedback. This allows them to convert theories and beliefs into facts by validating a problem or need, and then determining whether the business idea solves it. The formal methodology is called Customer Discovery, first developed by Steve Blank, a Silicon Valley entrepreneur and founder of the Lean Startup movement.

His Lean Launchpad class, taught by the National Science Foundation Innovation Corps (NSF I-Corps), has become the standard for the commercialization of federal research projects. Blank's approach centers on one important principle: there are no facts inside your building—you must get outside and talk directly with customers.

To effectively gather insights from customers, you need good questions. While there's clear advice on how to segment customers, qualify them, and capture feedback (via surveys, interviews, day-in-the-life observations, etc.), there's very little guidance as to *what* makes good questions.

Experts say good questions shouldn't be leading or biased. They say ineffective questions are those that are too broad or vague. They say effective questions are specific, but don't elicit just a "yes" or "no" answer. OK, that's all good and well, but here's where this advice becomes less helpful. Additional guidance includes "get facts, not opinions," "ask why to get real motivations," "adopt a beginner's mindset," and "ask if there's anything you should have asked but didn't."

There are no clear methods on *how* to craft questions.[1] More specifically, how to design questions to discover those unspoken needs—opportunities which neither the customer nor the organization can see. Ideally, this could be discovered through day-in-the-life observations. But not every circumstance easily allows this, especially in industries and environments which aren't typical consumer-product goods. In other cases, organizations may not have the resources or capabilities to go out in the field for deep-dive interactions. Interviews take time, and there's no clear way to speed up or optimize the process—yet.

Why It's So Hard

Processes are tools; the more you use them, the more adept you become. Yet traditional customer discovery isn't a formal process—only guidelines which suggest identifying customer problems, pain points, undesired costs (whether time or money), negative emotions (fears, risks, concerns), and where current solutions are underperforming (difficulties and challenges).[2] While

---

1. Crazy, I know. If you find any specifics, I'd love to hear them.

2. In short, figuring out what's keeping customers up at night and what's stopping them from making a change.

these guidelines seem straightforward, they are incredibly challenging in practice.

Imagine you're an executive at a bank, and you want to understand your customers' needs to develop new, differentiating financial products. You begin by gathering a team of department leaders
and discuss some initial ideas. The team shares their perspectives
on which of your bank's products are currently popular and maybe
some observations about what competitors are offering. You decide
it's important to get customer feedback and suggest conducting a
series of needs analyses and inquiries.

The team selects a few methods for capturing customer input
and, given limited resources, chooses a combination of online surveys and interviews. The surveys take a general temperature of
customer sentiment about services, products, and usage and solicit
some open-ended commentary on things like ATM availability and
elimination of additional fees. The interviews, on the other hand,
present a bigger hill to climb.

Initially, the team sorts through the customer database and
defines a cross section of individuals who represent different audience segments. Contact information is gathered, and an interview
schedule is established. Then it comes down (again) to what to ask.
Everyone has their own opinion and agenda. Some team members
want questions about specific competitor products and features.
Others want to ask customers for ideas on how they can improve
the bank's existing services. Cognitive biases, including bikeshedding and the curse of knowledge, set in.[3]

After extensive deliberation, a list of questions is finalized and
handed over to a few friendly and personable team members who
are good at talking with customers. The interviews are conducted,
and summaries are shared among the group. Disappointingly, the

---

3. See chapter two.

results don't uncover any magical or innovative ideas. Many customer comments reflect what was already captured in the online survey. The few nuggets of insight get promptly dismissed by the team (due to more cognitive bias). The conclusion is the interviews weren't very helpful, and the easiest solution is to just copy a competitor's popular offering.[4]

Why There's a Void

Does this sound all too familiar? Why did the interviews not reveal any epiphanies? What was missing? There's a lot to unpack in this scenario, but the core issue is perspective. The team was focusing on their own needs, interests, and wants. They approached interviews with a product-centered mindset, thinking about organizational offerings rather than the bigger challenges their customers were facing. The internally-focused mentality caused the team to ask the wrong questions, reinforcing status quo bias and reverting to a way-we've-always-done-it outcome.

Shifting that mindset takes more than a directive from organizational leadership because capturing useful customer insights is hard. Cognitive biases can cause interviewers to filter out lines of questioning, simply because of preconceived notions and assumptions. For example, a financial institution assumed their older clients wouldn't consider technology (digital and online tools) important on their list of needs. However, in a series of unbiased interviews, they found while older clients didn't often use technology themselves, they cared about it immensely. This was because their assistants used it and they equated a company having state-of-the-art technology as an up-to-date business.

---

4. I've honestly lived this a time or two before.

Uncovering those hidden needs is critical, as it can be the difference between creating unique differentiators versus weaker, duplicate offerings. It can be the difference between catapulting growth and remaining stagnant. It can be the difference between increasing competitiveness and getting slaughtered by market disruptors.

Uncovering Hidden Needs with 3W Ideation

I developed the 3W Ideation process from years of watching companies struggle to uncover opportunities that would catapult growth. I saw organizations of all sizes trying to get into the mindsets of their customers to no avail. I watched them wrestle with what questions to ask to discover hidden needs. Hence, a new process was born.

The 3W Ideation process helps you shift organizational mindsets to create a clear understanding of customer perspectives and contexts. In short, it helps you uncover customers' *whys* and *whats* to create a *wow* idea to take to market. Here's how it works:

Assemble a Group

Get in a room with a diverse group of five or so team members.[5] You'll need to have a broad range of individuals with varying backgrounds and personalities,[6] including analytical people, creative people, upper management, even interns. The more diverse, the better. The goal is to represent the widest range of perspectives and minimize groupthink behaviors.

---

5. Don't go too large—a room of fifty people will be hard to wrangle. Keep groups manageable.

6. Remember customer action learning?

Pick Your Query Subjects

When sales numbers miss their target or competitors start eating into market share, company leaders start putting on the pressure to get things turned around. Things are viewed as a "we need" problem: We need more sales. We need to be more competitive. We need innovations to better differentiate from competitors. Yet hyperfocusing on what *we* need prevents us from seeing what *customers* need. We need to tackle the problem from the customer's perspective.

The Query is the starting point for this mental shift. It is a tool to reframe your team's mindset away from internal needs to external opportunities. It creates a mental bridge between your current offerings and the larger environment that impacts and influences customer decisions.

The Query itself doesn't generate new product or service ideas (this comes later in the process) but does tee up a series of catalysts from which new opportunities are drawn. Your team can craft multiple queries to explore but should select one to pursue in depth. The Query structure consists of two simple parts: audience and offering.

3W Ideation Query

"Why would _____ (audience) want/need _____ (product/service offering)?"

Queries should be specific to one target audience (such as new parents) and specific to one existing offering (such as a baby monitor). This can be based on any criteria your organization deems most important, whether it be your most profitable products or a growing customer segment. No matter what combination you choose, this is your starting point for activating a cognitive shift.

Then Answer That Why

Once a Query is established, it's time to have the team start mentally putting themselves in the customers' shoes. This requires answering the Query you've formed.

Because we tend to be immersed in our own products and services, we have a hard time visualizing our customers' perspectives—that bigger context which influences their decision-making and where new differentiation opportunities lie. The Query provides a method to shift the team's attention to the circumstances that drive the needs posed by the Query. Let's consider one a financial institution used:

Query Example

"Why would **Millennials** (audience) want/need a **mortgage** (product/service offering)?"

Look how this Query alone starts changing your thinking. When we ask, "Why would Millennials want or need a mortgage?" it gets you considering catalysts—the impetus for action or behavior change—rather than solely the function of the product offering itself.

Even with a Query in place, you can still fall back to your old ways. In this example, the organization's gut reaction to this question was "to buy a house." However, this answer is simply a description of the product's function, much like potato chips satisfy hunger. The goal is to step back and examine the entire customer context, visualizing and identifying those reasons which may *cause* a Millennial to consider buying a home. Here's just a small cross section of catalysts the team came up with:

Ineffective Why Answer (Function)
- They need to buy a house

Effective Why Answers (Context)
- Got a new job across town
- Received a promotion
- Had/having a baby
- Want to leave a bad rental property
- Want to start a home-based business

Now we're cooking! While the bank initially was looking at the function alone (buying a house), by expanding their view, a list of catalysts and potential areas to serve the customer in new ways emerged.

Your team should come up with as many Why contexts as possible. Developing your list of Why contexts should take your group an hour or less. Each person should draw from their own life experiences to contribute to the list. Once created, the team can move on to the second W of the 3W Ideation process—the What.

Then Ask What

Here's where things get really interesting. Once we've established a solid understanding of the possible Why contexts, we can delve into the What elements. These are the things that impact, influence, and support the customer Why. What elements also may or may not be products or services you currently offer.

Your team should conduct a one- or two-hour brainstorming exercise to identify the widest range of What elements that possibly tie in to your Why contexts. For example, in our home-buying scenario, if a Why is "had a baby," their Whats may include help with moving, finding temporary childcare, or finding a home inspector. You can then narrow this list down based on what you believe fits your capabilities, how it differentiates you from competitors, and how it serves an unmet customer need. Let's look at some What elements with our Query example:

Query Example

"Why would **Millennials** (audience) want/need a **mortgage** (product/service offering)?"

Why Context Examples
- Got a new job across town
- Received a promotion
- Had/having a baby
- Want to leave a bad rental property
- Want to start a home-based business

What Needs Examples
- Help with moving
- Finding a home inspector
- Information on zoning laws
- Finding temporary childcare
- Getting construction permits

As you can tell, your What list can become quite extensive, especially if you have many Why contexts defined. You can select one or more Why contexts to create What element lists for, as needs can often overlap. Your What elements should also include emotional needs and obstacles, along with physical ones. For example, the Millennial might need expert counseling support in the more emotionally driven Why context of a spouse's passing. Thinking about the Whats in the broadest terms will give your team the best opportunity to create a comprehensive needs list. Now, let's see how it all comes together.

Conceive the Wow

Once your Why and What lists are created, your team can move on to developing a Wow hypothesis. The Wow hypothesis helps the team narrow their focus on a specific mix of contexts (Whys) and needs (Whats), creating a thesis for generating the most unique and impactful value for the customer (Wow). The Wow hypothesis is the foundation for implementing effective, targeted customer interviews. Interview questions should be utilized to either prove or disprove your Wow hypothesis. Here's an example Wow hypothesis using our example:

Query Example

"Why would **Millennials** (audience) want/need a **mortgage** (product/service offering)?"

Why Context
- Had/having a baby

What Needs/Obstacles
- Help with moving
- Finding a home inspector
- Finding temporary childcare

Wow Hypothesis Example
"New Millennial parents face a lot of challenges, and one of those is a securing a home for their growing family (Why context). Our hypothesis is there is a significant need for a concierge-style offering focused on helping them overcome moving preparation challenges and quickly acquire critical needs for relocation (What needs) creating a one-of-a-kind, seamless experience."

A Wow hypothesis is constructed in two parts. The first statement identifies the audience you're targeting and the Why you're examining. The second statement identifies the hypothesis you want to validate through customer interviews. Don't get lost in the

weeds on execution; focus on what you want to deliver in a way
that best fits what you perceive as the greatest opportunity for creating unique value.

Verify the Wow Hypothesis with the 3W Customer Interview Framework

Having shifted the team's mindset around the customer's context,
your interview questions can simply focus on confirming or dis-
affirming your Wow hypothesis. Often, a few targeted, in-depth
interviews can get you there. Most organizations only need feedback from approximately eighteen to twenty customers to uncover
most of the substantive information required. The quantity of
feedback required depends on your saturation point—the point at
which you can stop conducting interviews because you fail to hear
anything new.

A key part of verifying your hypothesis is understanding the
biggest influences on your customer perceptions and behaviors.
The 3W customer interview framework helps ensure you cover
those influences, specifically:

- Importance
- Efficiency
- Fulfillment
- Simplicity
- Frequency
- Intensity
- Urgency
- Affordability

The goal of this is to create a repeatable approach in which
responses can be easily compared, weighed, and sorted. Applicable in both B2B and B2C environments, the framework eliminates
unintentional discussion of product features, technology, pricing,

or purchase interest, all of which can generate misleading feedback. Here's how the eight influences translate into standardized interview questions:

3W Customer Interview Framework

Importance—How essential is this (for the customer)?
Efficiency—How valuable is this time (to the customer)?
Fulfillment—What is considered success (to the customer)?
Simplicity—How complex is this today (for the customer)?
Frequency—How often does this occur (for the customer)?
Intensity—How serious is this (for the customer)?
Urgency—How quickly should this be addressed (for the customer)?
Affordability—How cost sensitive is this (to the customer)?

Here's how the interview questions would be customized to fit our example Wow hypothesis:

Example Importance Question: "Can you tell me about what is (or might be) **important** to you in the process of getting a home?"
Example Efficiency Question: "Can you speak to how you utilize (or would utilize) your **time** when planning to get a new home?"
Example Fulfillment Question: "Can you tell me what you would consider **ideal outcomes** in the process of getting a new home?"
Example Simplicity Question: "Can you speak to what you find most **complicated or frustrating** about the process of getting a new home?"
Example Frequency Question: "Can you talk about **how often** you look for a new home?"
Example Intensity Question: "Can you tell me why the process of getting a new home would be **serious** to you?"

Example Urgency Question: "Can you talk about your most **urgent** needs when getting a new home?"
Example Affordability Question: "Can you talk about how you go about determining what's most **affordable** when getting a new home?"

When interviewing customers, concentrate on understanding the mentality behind their thoughts and feedback, exploring responses further by asking, "How so?" and "Why is that?" This enables you to gather a baseline of responses from the core questions plus supporting insights to clarify those perceptions. Your customer interviews can be as short as thirty minutes but may last as long as the customer is willing and able to contribute valuable feedback.

The 3W Ideation Process in Practice

If the process feels intimidating, try practicing it with another business before your own. Implement the process for something like a golf course, insurance company, or even a product manufacturer. The purpose of 3W Ideation is to establish a better understanding of customer environments, perceptions, and influences, and help prioritize areas where new value can be created.

Here's an example of the process in practice. A fencing manufacturer[7] was getting killed by subpar knockoffs, and their margins and market share were taking a major hit. Customers were viewing their fencing as simply a commodity and purchasing on price. The team was struggling to create new differentiators, so an internal 3W team was created to tackle the challenge.

---

7. Keeping things anonymous for privacy reasons.

They kicked things off by selecting a target audience that had the most growth potential. Through their own internal, validated analysis, they landed on one segment—middle-aged males. The team then selected a product that had the most dramatic decline in market share and was at most risk for disruption from competitors—their line of vinyl fencing.

The next step was creating their Query:

"Why would a **middle-aged man** want a **fence**?"

The team proceeded to create a Why list, defining all the possible contextual factors triggering their audience's need for a fence. This encompassed a wide range of unique ideas and perspectives:

Why
- Has/wants a dog that needs controlled space
- Wants privacy from the neighbors
- Has young children to keep safe from a high-traffic street
- Wants to increase home protection from theft
- Would be a nice aesthetic addition
- Establish property lines in a visual way
- Protect a garden from pests
- Increase the value of the property

After crafting the Why list, the team moved on to creating their What list, defining those customer needs which coincided with the contexts identified. Examples from their What list included the following:

What
- Understanding building codes
- Acquiring a building permit

- Getting underground lines flagged
- Having an assessor determine property lines
- Finding an installation contractor
- Laying out and measuring fence posts
- Determining style to fit their needs and aesthetics

Given the breadth of contextual factors, the team chose to narrow their focus on a handful of What elements. As a manufacturer, some ideas were not as appealing as others, and some were too far afield from their core capabilities.[8] This resulted in the creation of the following Wow hypothesis for customer validation:

Wow Hypothesis

"Middle-aged men seek to protect their privacy and physical assets on their property (Why context). Our hypothesis is to create modular, add-on security/privacy features, eliminating the need for permits, contractors, third-party or home-grown solutions (What needs), offering complete customization in a single package."

The Outcomes

Conducting seventeen customer interviews to verify their Wow hypothesis, the team found many customers felt the privacy a fence provided was incredibly important. Customers had also considered add-on security products, including lights and cameras. However, the unique enlightenment came when they questioned customers on simplicity. They discovered these middle-aged males were often not the final decision-makers. Their partners were influencing their choices, specifically the balance between security and aesthetic, and creating a lot of tension, disagreements, and

---

8. This enabled them to quickly filter their lists down to a reasonable size.

indecision. This previously undiscovered problem was the aha moment for the manufacturer.

In response, the team chose to create a prototype concept to test with customers. It was a modular panel that could be added or removed without tools to an existing fence structure, adding additional privacy and decoration simultaneously. The panels, with laser-cut design options, enabled customers to change the feel of a dated fence, or add flair to an existing framework, while also providing an additional layer of security.

After introducing the concept to key customers for further validation, the team launched the new offering with a variety of opaque, semitransparent, nontransparent, and even branded options (such as a favorite sports team logo). Each one could be mixed and matched depending on a customer's preference. Since launch,[9] the company has seen a 62 percent increase in revenues, with 51 percent constituting the new panel products.

Keys to Holding a 3W Ideation Workshop

Preparing for a 3W Ideation workshop requires minimal effort. Each team member should simply come with an open mind, without doing any advance research or other prework about perceived customer desires.

But let's be honest. Most workshops of any kind are flavored by office politics. High-powered stakeholders who are disconnected or unmotivated always affect a team dynamic. It's easy to end up with two or three people in the room who dominate the conversation and decisions.

So how do you ensure insight—not personal preference, power, biases, or emotion—drives ideas and prioritization? To be successful, teams must make hard decisions. They must leave their whims,

---

9. They were only six months postlaunch at the time this book was written.

tastes, and prejudices at the door. Something critical to one person may be insignificant to another. So how does your team come to a consensus on where to focus efforts? Diversified Voting.

Diversified Voting is where participants are assigned specific color markings (Post-its) to correspond to three key voting criteria—green for brand relevance, blue for financial viability, and red for technical or operational feasibility. Only a Wow hypothesis that gains majority votes from all three colors can be recognized as potentially profitable, feasible to implement, *and* relevant to the brand simultaneously. What ruins traditional voting is when leaders say, "Vote for what you like the most," or "Choose your favorite." These words give the team permission to fantasize and speculate. Don't do it. Diversified Voting delivers balanced, bias-free, rational selections.

Filtering of Truth

The goal of a 3W Ideation workshop should be to uncover those nuggets of truth—customer insights that reveal something innovative and revolutionary. But these nuggets must have two important attributes: useful and reliable. Useful means they provide clear opportunity and direction for next steps. Reliable means they are comprehensive, accurate, and reveal a consistent pattern. The best way to generate insights that meet both these criteria is through refinement and filtering of customer feedback.

When feedback is brought back for comparison against your Wow hypothesis, the team should discuss it in-depth, inquiring, "Why did the customer feel that way?" or "How do they currently handle that problem?" These exploratory questions will ensure the interviewer has captured all critical insights and help determine whether further interviewing is required. The objective is not "the more feedback, the better," but "the more useful and reliable, the better."

Familiar Can Be Blinding

When radio technology was first introduced in the early twentieth century, it was used only for transmitting Morse code. It was only after David Sarnoff suggested in 1915 it could be used for broadcasting news, music, and baseball games that the radio was born. Sarnoff spawned the idea when he observed families gathered in their homes and saw a different use for the technology. No one had asked for a radio because they didn't know it was feasible.

Sometimes we are so accustomed to the status quo, we're blind to opportunity. This causes us to push back against innovation, citing, "Customers haven't asked for that!" *Precisely.* By the time they do, competitors will have already launched the same idea, and you will become mired in a me-too game of copying and tweaking.

If you take nothing else from this chapter, remember that only by shifting mindsets can you begin to change the way your organization innovates. The 3W Ideation process is just a tool to help you on that journey.

9

Monetizing Customer Discoveries

Don't find customers for your products, find products for your customers.

—Seth Godin

Capturing actionable insights is only half the battle. Converting that feedback into new revenue streams is what creates organizational value, and that's where companies frequently fall short. While things like time, technology, money, and resource limitations can hamper the implementation of any idea, the reason they don't convert to revenue is often the lack of a clear monetization strategy. While it sounds cliché, organizations usually spend more time on brainstorming logos than how a validated hypothesis will convert to new revenue, new customers, or even increased share of wallet.

Revenue is frequently misunderstood, ignored, and neglected when converting innovation into profit (for the organization) and value (for the customers). Many executives still rely on their gut, believing *If we build it, they will come*, instead of creating a formal monetization plan. This causes the unintentional pursuit of strategies that directly, or indirectly, destroy value.

For example, a price promotion by a luxury brand designed to bring about new revenue might undermine the brand's premium positioning, eroding profits. Or a package redesign meant to generate more sales substantially increases costs. Or a new product introduction meant to create new customers results in cannibalizing revenue from other offerings.

Leaders often assume their accounting teams, who bring transparency to costs, can also provide clarity to revenue. Yet these two things are very different. Revenues are passive, often the indirect outcome of past activities. Costs are active, directly causing future ramifications. Cost is linear, while revenue is not. For example, a 10 percent increase in marketing costs may drive a 2 percent increase in revenue, but additional 10 percent increases in marketing spend are not guaranteed to generate additional 2 percent increases in revenue.

We need to think about monetization in a new way—embracing it as part of the ideation process, in which new products, services, and offerings can be brought to the table to benefit not only customers but also the organization's financial health.

What to think about through this chapter:

- Where to find sources of profit
- How to create a monetization strategy
- Why having a monetization expert is important

Finding Profit Sources

Creating a strategy resulting in revenue growth requires having a complete picture of all possible profit sources. This means understanding your industry's entire value chain and examining where opportunities can be found. By comparing these opportunities against your customer insights, your organization can create a direct connection between ideas and revenue.

U-Haul is a great example of an organization painting a full picture of profit sources. In the mid-1990s, U-Haul was the most profitable company in its industry, operating at a 10 percent margin—way above the 3 percent industry average. This profitability didn't come by accident. U-Haul studied its entire value chain, beyond its core truck-rental business, and identified a large, untapped source of profit—accessories. This included the sale of boxes, insurance, trailer rentals, and storage space.

U-Haul targeted these additional offerings because of observations and deep interactions with customers.[1] By uncovering hidden needs, they discovered what customers needed to accomplish their overarching objectives (e.g., moving to a new home, downsizing, and so on). With virtually no competition in the accessories space at the time, U-Haul could generate higher margins and differentiate themselves in a way that was meaningful for customers. Even though customers could source all their moving supplies from places like the post office or Staples, U-Haul centralized and simplified the process, enabling them to create completely new revenue streams.

When pursuing profit sources, there is also a cause-and-effect relationship to consider. In the automotive industry, for example, high margins in leasing can be a threat to used car profitability. As

---

1. Exactly the 3W Ideation process.

leased cars fill used car lots, the oversupply will likely erode prices, margins, and dealer profits. So, no approach is as straightforward as simply selecting the highest profit opportunity. By understanding what is most valuable to the customer, organizations can look beyond their day-to-day business, use 3W Ideation to uncover new opportunities, and determine which combination is best to pursue.

Creating a Monetization Strategy

Organizations often don't create a formal monetization strategy, and maybe it's because the word monetization can sound a bit sleazy. Maybe it comes off like a plan to dupe customers into paying for something they don't need, just to generate cash.

There are indeed many examples where companies have taken monetization too far, invading privacy or destroying trust, but that's monetization executed poorly. Monetization is about delivering meaningful value for customers and expecting to receive something in return—whether that's loyalty, repeat purchases, or new revenues.

Companies are in business to create growth, and even the most well-crafted, customer-focused initiatives cannot survive on good intentions alone. A simple monetization strategy can be architected using three steps: establishing viability, defining your get-keep-grow objective, and creating a revenue opportunity grid.

Step One: Establishing Viability

Determining the viability of your validated Wow hypothesis starts with having an agreed understanding of its key messaging, financial, and implementation elements. This requires the team to answer the following questions:

- How will customers perceive the new offering? (*Messaging*)
- Can customers afford to purchase at our required price point? (*Financial*)
- Can we gain a tangible competitive advantage? (*Implementation*)
- Can we generate repeat purchases, cross-selling, or upselling opportunities? (*Messaging*)
- Do the business economics of the offering work? (*Financial*)
- Can we deliver the offering reliably and at scale? (*Implementation*)

Clarifying these elements is essential. If the customer need is validated, but the organization cannot effectively implement the idea, justify the financials (for both the company and the customer), and create an appropriate messaging approach, outcomes will fall short of expectations. Determining these things up front will confirm the viability of the idea before moving forward.

Establishing viability should also include examining the activities of your competitors and potential competitors. Have other companies in the industry (or in other industries) implemented similar ideas? How did they approach it? Is there an opportunity to apply the idea both in our industry as well as others? Are there activities being performed in other industries that could displace or substitute this idea?

Step Two: Defining Your Get-Keep-Grow Objective

While a variety of approaches can generate revenue and profit, the most important part of your monetization strategy is to understand your get-keep-grow objective. With every Wow hypothesis, you can reasonably focus on only one of three objectives:

Are we trying to **get** new customers?

OR

Are we trying to **keep** existing customers?

OR

Are we trying to **grow** existing customers?

It's these objectives that can get the most muddied when crafting a monetization strategy. Frequently, teams try to do all of the above simultaneously with a single endeavor. While it might seem like a cure-all to achieve all three under one initiative, it is more advantageous to target a single, primary objective. For example, organizations waste a lot of time, money, and effort attempting to get new customers when they haven't developed a clear brand position or relationship with their existing audience.

Selecting a specific get, keep, or grow objective depends on your hypothesis. If the customer context, needs, and obstacles identified through the 3W Ideation process center on entirely new offerings, there could be opportunity to gain new customers. Ideas that reinforce and support existing offerings could be a way to retain and increase current customer loyalty.

In addition, the organization itself may have specific revenue generation needs to consider. If competing in a growing market, for instance, getting new customers might be most urgent. If serving an industry that has little differentiation between companies, a keep-and-grow strategy may be in order.

Step Three: Creating a Revenue Opportunity Grid

Once you have established viability and a get-keep-grow objective, the next step is to create a revenue opportunity grid. The grid helps ensure you understand and explore the four types of monetization possible for your Wow hypothesis: direct, indirect, ancillary, and partnership.

Customer Direct Revenue	**Customer Indirect Revenue**
Immediate revenue from a direct payment for a new product or service, whether onetime or recurring.	A no-cost product or service that generates downstream revenue in the form of other purchases.
Customer Ancillary Revenue	**Customer Partnership Revenue**
Direct revenue from the sales of products, services, or technologies to other companies or industries.	Working with a strategic partner to deliver offerings, generating revenue from other purchases.

These revenue channels can be used in combination or independently, depending on the scope of your Wow hypothesis. The goal is to make certain all avenues for revenue generation have been considered, and to identify which approaches best fit your get-keep-grow objective. Here's a simple illustration of each:

Customer Direct Revenue

Say a Wow hypothesis identifies the need for a new product or service offering. The company develops it, and customers purchase it for a specific dollar amount, whether onetime or recurring. For example, a bank may identify a segment of customers who need credit monitoring. A platform is developed, and customers subscribe to the service. This is customer direct revenue.

Customer Indirect Revenue

Perhaps a Wow hypothesis concludes customers need more comprehensive advice and information on choosing a product that's right for their needs. The company develops an online chat feature with live service personnel to help customers identify the right product, with the intent of converting those inquiries to downstream purchases. The support service is free, with the goal of future sales—an indirect source of revenue.

Company Ancillary Revenue

Suppose a Wow hypothesis reveals a unique, value-added offering for a call center serving catalog retailers—specifically, a differentiating method for managing telephone orders. The organization could offer this as a service to other industries outside of retail, creating an ancillary source of revenue.

Company Partnership Revenue

Consider a Wow hypothesis for a paint manufacturer that uncovers the disposal of leftover paint is a unique, unaddressed customer challenge. The manufacturer could develop a program in partnership with local hazardous-waste disposal companies to address the need without adding in-house resources or costs—increasing competitive differentiation and purchase preference.

How do we know which opportunity is best? It is a matter of thinking like a business owner and identifying all the ways revenue can be maximized, which usually isn't just one approach. For example, a new product can be sold directly to customers as well as indirectly to distributors. Or a value-added service a company isn't suited to implement themselves can be provided through a partner, generating opportunities to cross-sell or upsell supporting products. Or a capability that can be sold as a value-added service to other companies outside your industry. It's about finding and capitalizing on the best opportunities to generate revenue.

Notes on Pricing

Sometimes people want to distill monetization down to just pricing: lowering prices, raising prices, matching competitors' prices, and so on. But customers make purchase decisions by balancing their perceptions of price against value in complex, often subconscious ways. Contrary to popular belief, price is generally *not* the most important factor to customers when deciding to buy a product or service. The more a product or service is aligned with a specific customer's preferences and needs, the more it is valued.

The gap between what a customer is willing to pay and what they actually pay is the difference between value creation and appropriation. Value creation entails adding specific features and offerings that add value for the customer via a product or service. Value appropriation, on the other hand, is the value added through the buying experience itself. An example of this is Amazon's one-click purchasing, which allows customers to purchase through a single button, without having to reenter credit card, shipping, or contact information. The value appropriation here is making the purchase process incredibly simple, quick, and seamless. The experience itself creates value by reducing time, effort, and hassle.

You may develop a new offering and then attribute a value to it—what you believe the customer is willing to pay—and set a price to meet that expectation. However, more value—and, in turn, revenue—can be created when crafting memorable experiences and seamless processes around that product or service. This requires having a comprehensive understanding of customer perceptions, needs, obstacles, and context as captured through the

3W Ideation process. Keep in mind, there's not just one thing that creates customer value, just as there's not just one thing that determines a company's ability to appropriate value.

There's also not one pricing strategy suitable for all circumstances, and everyone on your team needs to conceptualize how the idea can make money, whether directly or indirectly. This may seem strange, but there's often a disconnect here. If team members don't understand how the organization makes money today, they're going to have a hard time envisioning how to translate new ideas into revenue. The effectiveness of any pricing strategy is the result of coordinated tactics working in tandem. Teams need to avoid getting tied up in justifying a single price point for an individual offering, and instead examine the entire monetization strategy itself.

Establishing a Monetization Leader

A good monetization strategy translates opportunities and approaches into actual projections and financial models. The costs of implementation of the idea must be considered, in addition to training, maintenance, and support where needed. In short, the idea must be translated into the language of business—numbers.

Establishing a head of monetization can help with this. They aid in defining ways to make your validated Wow hypothesis generate the best monetary value possible, including direct and indirect returns. They are responsible for finding ways to generate revenue and profit from new ideas but are often charged with creating it from something the organization already owns, whether it's a piece of land, a brand, or an advertising space on a blog. They are already present in many of today's industries, including tech companies, airlines, telecom, and even gaming.

This role, which can be at a manager, director, or even vice president level, typically leads the development of monetization approaches for all product and service offerings across the organization. They handle the design of formal business cases. They help teams understand and digest competitive research and customer feedback. They have strong analytical skills and a deep understanding of economics and pricing, in addition to a robust data modeling background.

Typically, new customer insights and new offering ideas are born from marketing, sales, customer service, or product-development teams, which usually aren't very experienced in finance, nor have a strategic revenue generation mentality. These teams have strong foundations in creativity, having full faith in the success of their ideas, whether validated from customer input or not. For example, an idea that customers say they don't need or want still might be pushed through by a team emotionally tied to it, despite contrary feedback. This is where a monetization leader can lend guidance—helping destroy their own and, more often, their team's bad ideas.

Why Not Use the Finance Team?

Some organizations believe financial departments can help with creating a monetization strategy, because they are more experienced with cost management and basic pricing models. But people in traditional finance roles are often ill-equipped to take on an endeavor of this magnitude.

They often aren't commercialization experts. They are classically trained in business finance, but frequently aren't trained to translate more abstract concepts into value, such as brand identity. They typically don't have broader reach and influence into departments beyond their own. They also are usually already overwhelmed with their existing responsibilities.

Without someone dedicated to examining the entire monetization picture, money will inevitably be left on the table.

Numbers Don't Explain Everything

The fact is, numbers never tell the whole story. In the 1960s, a group of economists did simple extrapolations of past costs in an attempt to predict the long-term program costs of Medicare. Their forecast was off by a factor of more than 1,000 percent, with actual costs being less than 10 percent of what was projected. Why?

Because the *human* factors weren't considered. The new Medicare program included financial incentives, encouraging innovation. New medicines were invented that reduced treatment costs. New treatments were developed as lower-cost remedies to specific health conditions. This is why the financial experts designed such an incorrect forecast—they oversimplified the context to get easy figures. They chose not to consider the contextual and behavioral effects of the people involved.

This same pitfall occurs in pricing strategies. Johnson Instruments[2] produced a unique safety device that, if it were to fail, could cause physical damage to the user, and major financial liability to the purchaser. They found the reason it was selling so poorly (even though it was higher quality than others on the market) was because it was priced significantly lower. The price made people perceive it as a low-quality offering, and therefore a high-risk purchase. They raised the price 30 percent, and sales volume increased forty-six-fold.

The perceived value of something also can depend on context. What is the value of a diamond versus the value of a bottle of water? Depending on the context, water may be much more valuable than a diamond—for example, if you're stranded in the desert.

If you take nothing else from this chapter, remember that many organizations struggle with monetization or simply don't know how to monetize new ideas. If you can't learn how to do it, hire someone who can help you establish a clear strategy for doing so.

---

2. Again, not their actual name.

10

Creating Customer Strategy Scorecards

The general who wins the battle makes many calculations in his temple before the battle is fought. The general who loses makes but few calculations beforehand.

—Sun Tzu

Measurement entails tracking how an initiative, project, or strategy is progressing, regressing, or simply changing. Peter Drucker famously said, "What gets measured gets managed," because what gets measured gets *noticed*. Employees naturally react to what their supervisors and managers are paying attention to. The problem is organizations, time and again, have misalignment between their commitments to stakeholders and the measures they use to track organizational performance.

Rio Tinto, one of the world's largest mining companies, stated in their 2020 annual report, "We work hard to understand our stakeholders' needs and expectations. We want our success to allow us to invest to meet our obligations to our employees, our customers, suppliers, local communities, and host governments, as well as to generate superior returns to our shareholders." Yet when it comes to their stated eight accountability measures in the same document, six are focused on shareholders and metrics around profit, one is focused on employee safety, and one is on greenhouse gases—the only one focused on local communities—and none on customers or suppliers.

Why the misalignment? If all stakeholders were as important as they claimed, Rio Tinto would logically have measurements to track organizational performance for all of them. In 2018, when Commonwealth Bank in Australia was investigated for financial misconduct, the oversight commission found the institution had given too little attention to monitoring organizational culture and overemphasized profit measurements. When we don't have measurements for customer goals (outside of profit metrics), we start to lose sight of customer and other stakeholder needs.

What to think about through this chapter:

- How to decide what to measure
- Why it's important to build a measurement architecture
- How to create a customer scorecard

Choosing What to Measure

What to measure is just as important as how it's measured. Einstein was quoted as saying, "Not everything that counts can be counted, and not everything that can be counted counts." We typically default to tracking things that are easy to measure, whether it be revenues, profit margins, or brand awareness. Most everyone is familiar with these measures, often referred to as key performance indicators, or KPIs.

However, KPIs only provide a surface view of organizational performance, lacking transparency to what drives growth or decline. If revenues are shrinking, for example, leaders will proclaim the organization needs to increase sales.[1] But what is the *cause*? Where is it happening? More importantly, how and where is the best place to try to increase sales? Increasing sales might not, in fact, be the sole solution.

Instead of measuring and tracking the *drivers* of revenue growth, the aggregate number is hotly discussed and debated. In one global manufacturing organization headquartered in the Midwest, during monthly revenue discussions, the executive vice president of sales would go around the room asking his district sales managers, "We need to increase sales. Anyone have opportunities or leads we can capitalize on?" This knee-jerk reaction could have been avoided by having more actionable measures in place from the get-go, such as customer attrition by geography and customer type, or sales decline and growth by product type.[2]

Having the right measures in place provides leaders the ability to understand organizational performance at a level that can be directly influenced. Choosing what to measure should be determined by three specific factors:

1. What adds value to **decision-making**
2. What adds value to **understanding performance**
3. What adds value to **improving outcomes**

For example, the number of downloads of an app might show a fair amount of people acquire the product but tells very little about how well the product is performing for those using it. Measuring your organization's number of social media followers says nothing

---

1. Of course!

2. For example, something like customer attrition, sliced by geography, industry, and product-purchase mix. Hell, anything would have been better than nothing.

about how many new customers are actually being acquired.[3] Measurements should measure something that matters to the business, and it's almost worthless to measure things you can't directly influence or that don't directly impact outcomes.

However, leaders continue to rely on poorly chosen measures. And they often use them to draw inaccurate conclusions, not realizing their intuition may be flawed. A fast-food chain thought lowering staff turnover would improve customer satisfaction and, in turn, profitability. "We just know this is the key driver," one executive explained. Confident in their intuition, they focused on reducing turnover. But to their surprise, some stores with high turnover were extremely profitable, while others with low turnover struggled. After further investigation, they found profitable stores had the strongest team leaders and managers, who quickly removed poor employees from the team, thus creating a high turnover number but also high customer satisfaction. Only when they shifted attention to this measure did they see a boost in satisfaction and profits.

As a business matures, measurements also need to shift accordingly to align with changing success objectives. For instance, a new wireless company entering the market might measure the acquisition rate of new customers. But as the company matures, it may need to shift emphasis from adding customers to better managing the ones it has, focusing on cross-selling or attrition reduction measures. Further issues will arise if cognitive biases and fixed mindsets inhibit such shifts in measurements, as they often do, causing organizations to end up managing the business with nonutilitarian metrics.

---

3. These are often referred to as "vanity metrics"—those that just make you feel good but have no value to business growth.

Determining Cause and Effect (Again)

In choosing what measures to track, it's critical to determine value-added objectives and the drivers which impact the creation of that value. Organizations frequently only measure objectives (such as customer satisfaction scores) without measuring the elements that drive them (such as repeat purchases).

While objectives can be easy to identify, determining their drivers is much more difficult. This is why organizations tend to stop exploration into drivers once the objective measures are determined. However, without drivers, it is almost impossible to identify the causal links between organizational initiatives and outcomes.

Selecting the right drivers requires meeting two criteria: they must be both predictable and effectible. A predictable driver impacts outcomes. An effectible driver is one you can influence. At a bank, a predictable driver for a customer satisfaction objective might be low teller turnover. The driver is also effectible because the organization can impact (increase or reduce) teller turnover.

Keep in mind, drivers should be continually reevaluated for their importance and relevance as the organization changes over time. Consider a bank's customer demographic that shifts over the years to a younger, more digitally savvy base. In this case, teller turnover might become less relevant, and digital interfaces might become more so. It's important to continually ensure you're not holding on to measures irrelevant to your current objectives.

Selecting the Right Objectives

Organizations can also cut corners when choosing objectives, often defaulting to overused KPIs borrowed from other companies within their industry. Having good objectives up front is critically important, as they drive all downstream actions and priorities for the organization. Bad objectives can't be tied to drivers—and in turn, initiatives—so there's little ability to understand what proverbial levers to pull to change the company's trajectory.

For example, an organization may believe customer satisfaction scores are a reasonable objective to have and measure. They track it monthly, checking to see if the number went up or down. But how does leadership know what's influencing that score? More importantly, do they know specifically what to do to influence it? Without understanding what drives and influences this measure, the objective is just a proxy for how well the company is performing for its customers.

A good objective is one that's measurable, directly influenceable, and impacts organizational performance. To determine if you have a good objective, answer these three key questions:

1.   What value does this objective provide to the **company**?
2.   What value does this objective provide to our **customers**?
3.   How do we **measure** success for the company and our customers?

An objective that effectively answers these questions provides an ideal platform on which to build drivers and initiatives. So instead of customer satisfaction scores, the company could use an objective such as customer retention, customer share of business, or even payment flexibility. In this scenario, let's use the objective of customer retention.

For the company, keeping a high level of retention directly impacts revenue and profits. For customers, retention ties directly to satisfaction, with their continuing use of a product or service.[4] Lastly, it's measurable because it can be clearly tracked.

The big difference between these types of objectives and traditional ones is context. Say a company believes their greatest strength is their breadth of product offerings, and creates an

---

4. Given it's not a monopoly-type situation.

objective focused on expanding and diversifying their product line. For customers, however, a more important objective might be on-time and reliable delivery. While the organization is focused on its product range, the customer need is in a completely different area. Expanding available products may even exacerbate underlying delivery problems rather than grow revenues.

This is why context is so important. Organizations can establish key objectives which may or may not create the outcomes they're looking to achieve. By creating objectives that directly impact employees, customers, and the company, organizations can create better drivers and initiatives that positively influence outcomes and, in turn, organizational performance.

Building a Measurement Architecture

Let's take a hypothetical example and walk through how basic objectives and drivers can be architected. Say a bank is looking to increase revenues, just as every other organization is seeking to do. Typically, tracking revenue growth would be the default measure because that's what the leaders are seeking to achieve. But this bank takes a different approach. Instead, they identify an objective—customer profitability—that directly impacts revenues and that they can measure and influence. This is followed by the identification of key drivers for the customer profitability objective, specifically additional product purchases. In this example, we'll use a loan product.

They follow this up with a series of 3W Ideation[5] exercises to determine why customers would purchase a loan, focusing on their most profitable customers.[6] Using their Wow hypothesis, they

5. Want a refresher on the 3W Ideation process? See chapter eight.
6. Instead of generic demographics such as age, gender, or occupation.

interview customers and find it's incredibly important to them to utilize their time efficiently.

The team then develops an initiative to make online loan applications faster and easier, creating a step-by-step question-and-answer process, walking customers through each decision they need to make. They integrate instant tips on how to make the best decisions for that individual's unique financial situation (such as the differences between a fixed and a variable rate loan). They also eliminate duplicate information across forms (including mailing address, social security number, etc.) to minimize the customer's time and effort.

Creating the Customer Strategy Scorecard

After establishing the approach, the team creates a Customer Strategy Scorecard, utilizing the objectives and driver previously defined, to design initiative metrics. Here's what their hypothetical scorecard architecture looks like:

Basic Customer Strategy Scorecard

Objective: Increase Customer Profitability			
Target Audience: High-Profit Customers without Loans			
Driver: Additional Product Purchases			
Initiative #1: Increase the Number of Loan Applications			
Current	Target	Timeline	Progress as of Feb
16 per month	30 per month	Jan–Sept	53% to goal

Keep in mind, scorecards can be presented in a variety of ways, whether with dials, line graphs, bar charts, or even an infographic. The goal is to ensure the information is presented in a clear, compelling way, articulating a succinct trend reflecting how the initiatives are either positively or negatively impacting objectives and drivers.

Not all scorecards need to look the same, and you should create a distinct scorecard for each of your organizational objectives. Depending on the drivers and initiatives for each objective, different types of measurements can and should be used.

Tracking individual initiative performance (on a weekly or monthly basis) can be part of the scorecard or a separate report, depending on the number of objectives, drivers, and initiatives you have. Additional information, such as qualitative feedback, is also excellent to add to your scorecard to help illustrate initiative performance and communicate customer input.

Your customer scorecards should also break out initiatives by target customer or prospect segment. Instead of taking a one-size-fits-all approach, targeting initiatives enables you to focus efforts and investment where there's the highest projected return. It also shows where things are performing according to plan and where they're not, providing the opportunity to reallocate resources more quickly to those initiatives that are performing successfully.

Dashboards versus Scorecards

Dashboards and scorecards are two terms often confused and used interchangeably. There are important differences between them. Both dashboards and scorecards make it easy to quickly find, analyze, and explore important data points. Deciding which to use depends on what metrics are being tracked and the goals associated with tracking the data.

Dashboards usually are a collection of graphs, charts, dials, or other visual elements used to monitor the levels of chosen metrics. They are mostly used for monitoring operational activities and are not necessarily directly linked with the strategic direction of a

company. In short, dashboards present a high-level idea of an organization's overall performance.

Scorecards, on the other hand, compare strategic goals with
results, typically showing a static view of an organization at one
point in time. Scorecards help you identify the gap between current performance and the goal. They help you track the progress of
a set strategy, measuring the effectiveness of initiatives, indicating
problems, and identifying solutions.

In essence, the difference between dashboards and scorecards is that scorecards focus on a specific metric against a target,
whereas dashboards present trends at a high level. Nick Khawaja,
writing for his personal blog, summarized it best: "In short, a dashboard is a performance monitoring system, whereas a scorecard is
a performance management system."

He states, "Scorecards are ideal when needing a concise view of
a specific area. If you need to determine how a specific team is han-
dling their initiatives, a scorecard can illuminate how close or far
they are from their goals. This can be useful when you're attempting to identify areas for improvement or ways to increase efficiency.
Dashboards are advantageous when you need a bird's eye view of
overall operations. Instead of specifically tracking progress toward
goals, dashboards deliver a better view of historic progress."

In short, dashboards and scorecards can be used together, but
scorecards link objectives to specific causes and effects. They provide insight beyond "we're doing better" or "we're doing worse." But
what's the value of a performance metric if you don't have insight
as to what's influencing it?

The Impact of Metrics on Behaviors

Companies can easily lose sight of objectives, focusing strictly on
metrics meant to represent them. The tendency to mentally replace
objectives with metrics—called *surrogation*—is quite pervasive.

When employees are incentivized and compensated by metrics alone, they do whatever is necessary to achieve those numbers. With the wrong measures, there can be unintended consequences.

For example, surgical performance is often measured by how often there are complications or deaths on the operating table, both of which impact doctor reputation and hospital marketability. Unintended, negative results of this type of measure might be surgeons refusing to take high-risk or complicated cases, resulting in patients who need help getting inferior care. A better measure would incorporate a difficulty, risk, or complication rating into the performance calculations, creating a more balanced comparison. Or consider sales teams who are measured on the number of leads they generate. This frequently results in tons of poor, unqualified leads, sucking up time and resources that could have been applied elsewhere.

Metrics are often given little thought; we base their selection on what we want to achieve. Metrics should not be in place simply to measure performance, but to help make better decisions. They should enable an organization to clearly understand what's working, what's not, and why.

Say your product is meeting its revenue and profit goals, and customer engagement and referral rates are high. This seems to suggest things are going well. But if at the same time, organizational morale is low and product quality is deteriorating, then there is cause for concern. Even though the revenue and profit metrics are undoubtedly important, they are not sufficient for painting the full picture of a company's health. Measures aren't just numbers—they reflect your company's vision, priorities, and focus.

A Closing Note on Thinking and Questioning

We can get easily overwhelmed with the day-to-day. But taking time to think—to ask the right questions when faced with challenges—is essential for connecting ideas to tangible and, more importantly, successful outcomes. However, many of the approaches and methodologies organizations often turn to eliminate rather than foster critical thinking.

Canned processes tell us *what* to think. That is, they provide us with rote procedures to follow to accomplish a task. They provide very little insight to the *why*. With a steady diet of this linear structure, it's no wonder we have a hard time getting people to be as passionate, creative, and innovative as they can be.

We need to focus on helping teams not just learn *what* to think, but *how* to think. Learning how to think opens new mental doors. If we teach employees what to think, they take what they know and just apply it to similar situations. Yet if we teach employees how to think, they can take that same knowledge and elegantly apply it to varying situations and scenarios.

When faced with large amounts of information or real-world problems rather than theoretical ones, those who have only been told *what* to think resort to guessing. We give these people more data, more tools, and more choices, but decision-making doesn't improve—it gets worse.

If everyone isn't on the same page with the organization's objectives, this fragmentation accelerates further. Take, for example, an objective of organizational growth. What does that mean to all the stakeholders involved? Revenue growth? People growth? Market share growth? Without clarity and specificity to objectives—and pairing them with actionable drivers—there's misalignment on both directing efforts and uncovering possible solutions.

Those people who know how to think can effectively ask questions by suspending their judgments and assumptions just long enough to understand someone else's perspective, thus creating new ways of thinking about a problem. This type of deep questioning reduces group conflict, helps develop a common language, and establishes a shared vision. Those who know how to think and ask questions naturally evolve their thought processes as situations or circumstances change.

This skill is essential for creating and driving any change within an organization—especially the ones discussed in this book. Asking good questions as a means of looking beyond what's seen and understood on the surface. Asking good questions to shift mindsets from automatic, reactionary thinking to critical thinking. Asking good questions to fuel passion, enable innovation, and spur action.

Good questioning isn't shaped by a subject or idea, but by the words we choose. How we phrase and present questions differentiates a good question from a bad one. It's the difference between asking what we *should* do versus what we *could* do. It's a shift from thinking in limitations to thinking in opportunities.

We've been taught what to think for so long that the idea of asking questions that require critical thought is often hard to digest. Questions can create fear, doubt, anxiety, and stress—all of which are natural, biological reactions to dealing with uncertainty. These feelings can impede and impair learning. They can also suppress our ability to connect and listen to other people's perspectives. But good questions will expose our biases, surface our true viewpoints, and enable actual learning to take place.

Ask questions that inspire others to think about what they *could* do, not just what they *should* do. In an era where all the answers to our business challenges are seemingly at our fingertips, the real talent lies in being able to ask good questions. And we all need to get better at asking them.

EPILOGUE

Beethoven became a more brilliant composer as his ability to hear deteriorated. He became less influenced by prevailing musical trends and more moved by the unique ideas formed inside his head. His early work was reminiscent of the style of his instructor and teacher, Josef Haydn. Beethoven's later work became so original that he became regarded as the father of music's Romantic period. Deafness freed Beethoven as a composer because he was no longer limited by the influences of others.

While we are continually bombarded by all the noise within our organizations—from customers, bosses, vendors, and shareholders—we cannot lose the ability to see beyond the here and now. We can't lose sight of the value of challenging the status quo, reflecting on what could be, and confidently pushing innovative change.

Yeah, yeah. That's lovely, inspirational commentary. But the real world is another thing entirely. Certain shareholders' voices can ring much louder and stronger than customers' do. Bosses can make demands counterintuitive to proven insights or data points, throwing around their HIPPO power.[1] While we continue to beat the drum on customer needs and voice, companies continue to

---

1. Termed by Adam Grant, the highest paid person's opinion, which can carry more weight than facts.

disregard it. Internal politics get in the way. Fear gets in the way. Risk aversion gets in the way.

But as the famed journalist Hunter S. Thompson said, "Anything worth doing is worth doing well." It's not easy to push back against an organization that has succumbed to inertia. It's not easy to change long-embedded mindsets and perspectives. It's not easy to maintain focus and persistence, to achieve goals that don't deliver immediate results. But it's worth doing, and it's worth doing well.

This book shouldn't be considered a cure-all, but a starting point—the beginning of a transformation that will take time and repetition to fully achieve. We all have gone through transformations in our business lives, many of which we readily forget. We forget the time when we were starting our careers with vim and vigor, full of ideas and initiative. We forget how we saw obvious and often simple ways for the organization to change, from streamlining a process to simplifying a customer experience. We forget our frustrations as customers, when we had to navigate multilevel, automated phone trees, or endless redundancy when trying to cancel a subscription service.

These experiences aren't lost, just left behind. As we become indoctrinated into our organizations, we lose sight of those small but important things. Like a racehorse with blinders, we barrel straight down the track to the finish line, without consideration for the environment around us. We get mired in what *we* want to achieve, what *we* want as outcomes, what *we* want to see happen. But none of those things can happen—whatever they may be—without customers. Customers are not businesses or things; they are people. People who must make decisions, weigh options, and who share many of the same fears, frustrations, and concerns we do.

Action over Platitudes

There's a legendary phrase commonly used among C-suite leaders, customer service reps, and venture capital firms: "Let me know how I can be helpful." It's so common it's become a meme, precisely because it's *not* helpful. It sounds supportive but does nothing. Organizations need to relearn how to be helpful.

It's astonishing how much casual, drive-by advice occurs. Being helpful in tone is not the same as being helpful in action. We can think we're adding value when nitpicking or supplying unsolicited commentary when, instead, we're draining energy and momentum. To truly help our organizations, our customers, and even ourselves, we must *act*. We need to be makers. We need to be doers.

One of the things they teach you as a lifeguard is that people who are drowning will attempt to climb on top of their rescuers, potentially killing both. Similarly, simply trying to help solve a problem in an organization can expose vulnerabilities both in the organization and the individual. Many people just avoid helping altogether and hunker down for personal safety. Those who attempt it can end up battle-scarred from fending off complaints and criticisms. But again, this doesn't mean it isn't worth doing.

Our biggest challenge in business isn't building up the gumption to act but dealing with the mindsets of people and their resistance to change until circumstances force them to. In times of prosperity, it's not easy to understand why change is needed now; yet the best generator of long-term success is doing things when we don't feel like doing them.

Now is the time to make the conscious decision to act. Be curious. Ask why. Be helpful. This goes for both customers and employees. Remember, human beings are creatures of mimicry. Fearlessly embody the behaviors and mindset you want to see, and others will follow. No book, process, or methodology can make that happen, though they can look great on your bookshelf. Don't let this be another one of those casualties of intent without action.

ACKNOWLEDGMENTS

First and foremost, I want to give a huge thanks to my husband, Tim. While you may not have provided advice on content (or even read the book yet), you delivered unwavering support and patience for my hundreds of days and nights of keyboard tippity-taps.

I also want to thank my mother, Leslie, and my late father, Darwin, for instilling the confidence and work ethic necessary to persevere through self-doubt, and the tenacity to always question the status quo.

I would be remiss if I didn't thank those great minds that have inspired so many of the concepts found in these pages, including Roger Martin, Dr. Graham Kenny, Shane Parrish, Richard Shotton, Rory Sutherland, and Simon Sinek. Your insights and perspectives are invaluable.

Lastly, I'd like to give my endless gratitude to the entire Ben-Bella team (Katie, Brigid, Mallory, Jay, Alicia, and Aida) for an amazing experience throughout the entire publishing process, and a special tip-of-the-hat to Matt Holt for taking a chance on an unknown author.

BIBLIOGRAPHY

Adcock, Phillip. "What Is Salience Bias?" Adcock Solutions. March 21, 2021. https://www.adcocksolutions.com/post/what-is-salience-bias.

Alvarez, Cindy. *Lean Customer Development: Building Products Your Customers Will Buy.* O'Reilly, 2017.

Andrade, Goncalo. "Learning Cards: Organizing Research Findings in an Easily Digestible Format." UX Collective. December 16, 2019. https://uxdesign.cc/learning-cards-bf7fb204d2f6.

Andrus, Jeremy. "Trager's CEO on Cleaning Up a Toxic Culture." *Harvard Business Review.* March 2019. https://hbr.org/2019/03/traegers-ceo-on-cleaning-up-a-toxic-culture.

Anthony, Scott. "The Five Cs of Opportunity Identification." *Harvard Business Review.* October 26, 2012. https://hbr.org/2012/10/the-five-cs-of-opportunity-identi.

Ashworth-Keppel, Tanya. "Four Cognitive Biases That Affect Your Leadership." *Australian Institute of Business.* December 21, 2018. https://www.aib.edu.au/blog/leadership/four-cognitive-biases-that-affect-your-leadership/.

Auerbach, David. "How Facebook Has Flattened Human Communication." Medium. August 28, 2018. https://onezero.medium.com/how-facebook-has-flattened-human-communication-c1525a15e9aa.

Bailey, Catherine. "External Perspective—An Under-Utilized Strategic Leadership Capability." Springerlink. 2008. https://link.springer.com/chapter/10.1057/9780230584075_3.

Bariso, Justin. "Amazon Has a Secret Weapon Known as 'Working Backwards'— and It Will Transform the Way You Work." *INC.* March 23, 2021. https://www.inc.com/justin-bariso/amazon-uses-a-secret-process-for-launching-new-ideas-and-it-can-transform-way-you-work.html.

Barlow, Buckley. "Uncovering an Innovative Monetization Strategy to Keep Your Organization Relevant." Rocket Source. April 14, 2021. https://www.rocketsource.co/blog/monetization-strategy/.

Barney, Josh. "Context in Marketing: Decision-Making, Influence, and Broken Windows." Einstein Marketer. January 22, 2021. https://www.einsteinmarketer.com/context-marketing/.

Bartlett, Christopher. "Rebuilding Behavioral Context: Turn Process Reengineering into People Rejuvenation." MIT *Sloan Review*. October 15, 1995. https://sloanreview.mit.edu/article/rebuilding-behavioral-context-turn-process-reengineering-into-people-rejuvenation/.

Bean, Randy. "Why Is It So Hard to Become a Data-Driven Company?" *Harvard Business Review*. February 5, 2021. https://hbr.org/2021/02/why-is-it-so-hard-to-become-a-data-driven-company.

Beaubien, Rhiannon. "Academic Economics: Strengths and Weaknesses, Considering Interdisciplinary Needs by Charlie Munger." *Farnam Street*. 2003. https://fs.blog/great-talks/academic-economics-charlie-munger/.

———. "Common Probability Errors to Avoid." *Farnam Street*. 2020. https://fs.blog/2020/11/common-probability-errors/.

———. "First Principles: The Building Blocks of True Knowledge." *Farnam Street*. 2018. https://fs.blog/2018/04/first-principles/.

———. "How Julia Child Used First Principles Thinking." *Farnam Street*. November 2020. https://fs.blog/2020/11/how-julia-child-used-first-principles-thinking/.

———. "The Munger Two Step." *Farnam Street*. April 2013. https://fs.blog/2013/04/munger-two-step/.

———. "The Psychology of Human Misjudgment by Charlie Munger." *Farnam Street*. January 3, 2020. https://fs.blog/great-talks/psychology-human-misjudgment/.

———. "The Work Required to Have an Opinion." *Farnam Street*. April 2013. https://fs.blog/2013/04/the-work-required-to-have-an-opinion/.

———. "Your Environment Shapes Your Decisions." *Farnam Street*. December 2013. https://fs.blog/2013/12/your-environment-matters/.

Becker, Gregor. "Behavioral Science in Insurance—Nudges Improve Decision Making." McKinsey and Company. September 21, 2020. https://www.mckinsey.com/industries/financial-services/our-insights/insurance-blog/behavioral-science-in-insurance-nudges-improve-decision-making.

Berg, Paul. "Why Banks and Credit Unions Keep Blowing It Using Net Promoter Scores." The Financial Brand. October 19, 2020. https://thefinancialbrand.com/91258/net-promoter-score-customer-engagement-performance-metrics/.

Berger, Jonah. "How to Persuade People to Change Their Behavior." *Harvard Business Review.* April 20, 2020. https://hbr.org/2020/04/how-to-persuade-people-to-change-their-behavior.

Bersin, Josh and Marc Zao-Sanders. "Making Learning a Part of Everyday Work." *Harvard Business Review.* February 19, 2019. https://hbr.org/2019/02/making-learning-a-part-of-everyday-work.

Biggs, Michael. "Prophecy, Self-Fulfilling/Self-Defeating." *Encyclopedia of Philosophy and the Social Sciences.* Sage, 2013.

Blank, Steve. "Are You Solving Customer Problems?" September 5, 2014. YouTube video. https://www.youtube.com/watch?v=spcJYXS7T84.

Blum, Andrew. "How a $4000 Vet Bill Sparked Innovation at American Express." IDEO. 2017. https://www.ideo.com/case-study/how-a-4000-vet-bill-sparked-innovation-at-american-express.

———. "How One Human-Centered Insight Led to $4 Billion in Growth for American Express." IDEO. December 17, 2020. https://www.ideo.com/journal/how-one-human-centered-insight-led-to-4-billion-in-growth-for-american-express.

Bonny, Clive. "Applying Action Learning to Design and Deliver Customer Service." Strategic Management Partners. January 6, 2021. https://consult-smp.com/archive/2007/01/applying-action-learning-to-design-and-deliver-customer-service.html.

Brooks, Arthur. "This Holiday Season, We Can All Learn a Lesson from Beethoven." *Washington Post.* December 13, 2019. https://www.washingtonpost.com/opinions/this-holiday-season-we-can-all-learn-a-lesson-from-beethoven/2019/12/13/71f21aba-1d0e-11ea-b4c1-fd0d91b60d9e_story.html.

Brown, Linden. "Diagnose Your Customer Culture." *Harvard Business Review.* January 17, 2014. https://hbr.org/2014/01/diagnose-your-customer-culture.

Brown, Tristam. "Are the Best Company Cultures Internally or Externally Focused." LSA Global. March 16, 2021. https://lsaglobal.com/blog/are-the-best-company-cultures-internally-or-externally-focused/.

Brownlow, Taylor. "Dashboards are Dead." Toward Data Science. April 9, 2020. https://towarddatascience.com/dashboards-are-dead-b9f12eeb2ad2.

Brownwell, Matt. "The WebMD Effect: Most Americans Are 'Cyberchondriacs.'" The Street. September 19, 2011. https://www.thestreet.com/personal-finance/insurance/webmd-effect-most-americans-are-cyberchondriacs-12789860.

Bruun, Morten. "The (Real) Secret Formula of McKinsey." Medium. January 7, 2021. https://medium.com/@mortenbbruun/the-real-secret-formula-of-mckinsey-ff50d65e70a7.

Burkhardt, John. "Behavioral Inertia: The Low Cost of Doing Nothing." LinkedIn (blog). November 14, 2019. https://www.linkedin.com/pulse/inertia-low-cost-doing-nothing-john-burkhardt-ph-d-/.

Butman, John. "Seven Tips for Shifting a Mindset in Your Organization." *Harvard Business Review.* August 12, 2013. https://hbr.org/2013/08/how-to-shift-a-mindset-in-your.

Byrnes, Jonathan and John Wass. "How Midsize Companies Can Use Data to Compete with Digital Giants." *Harvard Business Review.* February 22, 2021. https://hbr.org/2021/02/how-midsize-companies-can-use-data-to-compete-with-digital-giants?utm_campaign=hbr&utm_medium=social&utm_source=linkedin.

Camp, Jim. "Decisions Are Largely Emotional, Not Logical." *BigThink.* June 11, 2012. https://bigthink.com/experts-corner/decisions-are-emotional-not-logical-the-neuroscience-behind-decision-making.

Campbell, A. J. "Creating customer knowledge competence: Managing customer relationship management programs strategically." *Industrial Marketing Management.* 2003.

Cancel, David. "A Simple Framework for Handline Customer Feedback." Drift. September 13, 2016. https://www.drift.com/blog/customer-feedback-framework/.

Carrel, Alexis. *Man, The Unknown.* New York: Harper & Brothers, 1939.

Cattin, Christy. "How to Explore the Problem Space with Your Team." Medium. June 25, 2020. http://webcache.googleusercontent.com/search?q=cache:7sbFzsitK-0J:https://medium.com/@christycattin/how-to-explore-the-problem-space-with-your-team-c6d400c0278c&hl=en&gl=us&strip=1&vwsrc=0.

Cavanaugh, Emily. "Parents in Nordic Countries Have Their Babies Nap Outside in Subzero Temperatures So They Sleep Longer and Better." Insider. January 30, 2020. https://www.insider.com/nordic-parents-nap-babies-subzero-temperatures-sleep-better-2020-1.

Chadwick, Peter. "Action Learning Explained." IEDP. January 10, 2017. https://www.iedp.com/articles/action-learning-explained/.

Chambers, Sarah. "Who Should Be Accountable for Customer Feedback Loops?" Kayako. October 24, 2017. https://www.kayako.com/blog/customer-feedback-loop/.

Chase, Richard and Sriram Dasu. "Want to Perfect Your Company's Service? Use Behavioral Science." *Harvard Business Review.* June 2001. https://hbr.org/2001/06/want-to-perfect-your-companys-service-use-behavioral-science.

Cherry, Kendra. "The Affect Heuristic and Decision Making." Very Well Mind. May 7, 2020. https://www.verywellmind.com/what-is-the-affect-heuristic-2795028.

Ciotti, Gregory. "10 Unforgettable Customer Service Stories." HelpScout. January 22, 2021. https://www.helpscout.com/10-customer-service-stories/.

———. "Why Steve Jobs Didn't Listen to His Customers." HelpScout. March 6, 2013. https://www.helpscout.com/blog/why-steve-jobs-never-listened-to-his-customers/.

Clear, James. "First Principles: Elon Musk on the Power of Thinking for Yourself." JamesClear. December 7, 2020. https://jamesclear.com/first-principles.

———. "Forget About Setting Goals. Focus on this Instead." JamesClear. 2019. https://jamesclear.com/goals-systems.

Cocheo, Steve. "6 CX Developments Banks and Credit Unions Can't Ignore in 2021." The Financial Brand. December 7, 2020. https://thefinancialbrand.com/104188/customer-experience-cx-digital-innovation-itm-telehealth-curbside-drivethrough-covid-19-pandemic-coronavirus-design/?edigest.

———. "Why Bankers Are So Disappointed by the ROI of Marketing Data and Analytics." The Financial Brand. November 12, 2020. https://thefinancialbrand.com/103624/marketing-data-analytics-scientist-digital-innovation-trend/?edigest.

Colao, J.J. "Steve Blank Introduces Scientists to a New Variable: Customers." Forbes. August 1, 2012.

Cone, Taylor. "What's Next for Design Thinking." Medium. June 2, 2019. https://modus.medium.com/whats-next-for-design-thinking-d44bebbb7649.

Connor, Tom. "Plan Continuation Bias." Medium. October 8, 2020. https://medium.com/10x-curiosity/plan-continuation-bias-60efcc2b4cbe.

Cook, Andy. "4 Cognitive Biases That Stop You from Scaling Your Business." Tettra. January 25, 2020. https://tettra.com/article/cognitive-biases-stopping-you-from-scaling-your-business/.

Copi, I.M., Cohen, C., Flage, D.E. Essentials of Logic, 2nd Ed. Upper Saddle River: Pearson, 2006.

Corkindale, Gill. "The Importance of Organizational Design and Structure." Harvard Business Review. February 11, 2011. https://hbr.org/2011/02/the-importance-of-organization.

Cornfield, Gene. "The Most Important Metrics You're Not Tracking (Yet)." Harvard Business Review. April 30, 2020. https://hbr.org/2020/04/the-most-important-metrics-youre-not-tracking-yet.

Cowan, Alexander. "Yellow Walkman Data and the Art of Customer Discovery." AlexanderCowan. September 9, 2020. https://www.alexandercowan.com/yellow-walkman-data-art-of-customer-discovery/.

Crogan, Mary. "2014 Wasting Time at Work Survey." Salary. March 19, 2014. https://www.salary.com/chronicles/2014-wasting-time-at-work/.

Cross, Robert. "Customer-Centric Pricing: The Surprising Secret for Profitability." SlidePlayer. 2015. https://slideplayer.com/slide/10098681/.

Cummins, Denise. "How to Get People to Change Their Minds." *Psychology Today.* February 25, 2016. https://www.psychologytoday.com/us/blog/good-thinking/201602/how-get-people-change-their-minds.

D'Ambrosio, Cecilia. "75+ Inspirational Quotes on Customer Centricity." iCity Magazine. April 3, 2017. https://tenfore.nl/blog/inspirational-quotes-on-customer-centricity/.

D'avila, Bettina. "Reframing the Problem." Medium. January 22, 2019. https://medium.com/nyc-design/reframing-the-problem-200f6c966dfc.

Daffy, Chris. "Five Reasons Why Many CX Journey Maps Fail to Generate Worthwhile Results." MyCustomer. https://www.mycustomer.com/experience/engagement/five-reasons-why-many-cx-journey-maps-fail-to-generate-worthwhile-results.

Davenport, Thomas and Leandro DalleMule. "Know What Your Customers Want before They Do." *Harvard Business Review.* December 2011. https://hbr.org/2011/12/know-what-your-customers-want-before-they-do.

Davey, Neil. "Seven Common Customer Journey Mapping Mistakes to Avoid." MyCustomer. February 14, 2020. https://www.mycustomer.com/customer-experience/engagement/seven-common-customer-journey-mapping-mistakes-to-avoid.

De Paula, Matthew. "2019 Reputation Survey: Can Banks Stop the Slide." American Banker. June 25, 2019. https://www.americanbanker.com/news/bank-reputation-survey.

Deal, David. "How Netflix Is Changing Your Behavior." Medium. July 20, 2018. https://davidjdeal.medium.com/how-netflix-is-changing-the-world-ddc2708f2063.

Deasi, Gary. "7 Huge Common Misconceptions about Customer Journey Mapping." Customer Journey Marketer. September 20, 2016. http://customerjourneymarketer.com/customer-journey-mapping-misconceptions/.

DeLamater, John D. and Daniel Myers. *Social Psychology, 6th Ed.* Belmont: Thomson Wadsworth, 2007.

DeMars, Regina. "5 Ways FNBO Engages Millennials and Gen Z with Content." The Financial Brand. January 14, 2021. https://thefinancialbrand.com/98465/social-media-trends-millennials-generation-z-gen-debit-card/?edigest.

Dholakia, Paul and Vicki Morowitz. "How Surveys Influence Customers." *Harvard Business Review.* May 2002. https://hbr.org/2002/05/how-surveys -influence-customers.

Di Fiore, Alessandro. "How to Keep Employees Connected to Customers." *Harvard Business Review.* June 21, 2019. https://hbr.org/2019/06/how-to-keep -employees-connected-to-customers.

Doneva, Radina. "How to Apply Behavioural Economics to the Design Process." Medium. June 5, 2018. https://radinadoneva.medium.com/how -to-apply-behavioural-economics-to-the-design-process-8eb9458 bec62.

Dongala, Mathilde. "Analysing Data and Generating Insights from User Interviews Using Tags." Medium. October 29, 2020. https://uxrw.medium.com /analysing-data-from-users-interviews-using-tags-86908a9b9d0e.

Dzekman, Rick. "4 Methods for Analyzing User Interviews." RickDzekman. September 30, 2019. http://webcache.googleusercontent.com/search?q =cache:eVkjhC0YYHIJ:https://rickdzekman.com/thoughts/4-methods -for-analysing-user-interviews/&hl=en&gl=us&strip=1&vwsrc=0.

———. "UX Research: Objectives, Assumptions, and Hypothesis." RickDzekman. September 21, 2019. http://webcache.googleusercontent.com /search?q=cache:ggGiBKLQze8J:https://rickdzekman.com/thoughts/ux -research-objectives-assumption-and-hypothesis/&hl=en&gl=us&strip =1&vwsrc=0.

Ellenberg, Jordan. "Abraham Wald and the Missing Bullet Holes." Medium. June 14, 2016. https://medium.com/@penguinpress/an-excerpt-from -how-not-to-be-wrong-by-jordan-ellenberg-664e708cfc3d.

Erickson, Tamara and Lynda Gratton. "What it Means to Work Here." *Harvard Business Review.* March 2007. https://hbr.org/2007/03/what-it-means -to-work-here.

Eschenroder, Kyle. "10 Overlooked Truths About Taking Action." The Art of Manliness. April 30, 2020. https://www.artofmanliness.com/articles/10 -overlooked-truths-about-taking-action/.

Faudree, Melissa. "The Seven Eras of Marketing." GetSimple. October 3, 2016. https://www.getsimple.com/blog/seven-marketing-eras/.

Ferrazzi, Keith. "Managing Change, One Day at a Time." *Harvard Business Review.* July 2014. https://hbr.org/2014/07/managing-change-one-day-at -a-time.

Fish, Jefferson. "Cultural Misunderstandings." *Psychology Today.* May 25, 2010. https://www.psychologytoday.com/us/blog/looking-in-the-cultural -mirror/201005/cultural-misunderstandings.

Flora, Carlin. "The Art of Influence." *Psychology Today.* September 6, 2011. https://www.psychologytoday.com/us/articles/201109/the-art-influence.

Flovik, Vegard. "The Hidden Risk of AI and Big Data." Toward Data Science. August 14, 2019. https://towarddatascience.com/the-hidden-risk-of-ai-and-big-data-3332d77dfa6.

Flowers, Eric. "The 'Job' to Be Done Is Never What You Think." Practical Service Design. December 16, 2016. https://blog.practicalservicedesign.com/the-job-to-be-done-is-never-what-you-think-d019bc16bc95.

Flynn, Bill. "How Expedia Saved $100M by Looking Upstream." Catalyst Growth Advisors. August 4, 2020. https://catalystgrowthadvisors.com/2020/08/04/how-expedia-saved-100m-by-looking-upstream/.

Force, Chris. "Paul Wraith on the Human-Centered Design Behind the New Ford Bronco." Sixtysix. December 22, 2020. https://sixtysixmag.com/paul-wraith/.

Forsey, Caroline. "Goals vs Objectives: The Simple Breakdown." HubSpot. April 24, 2019. https://blog.hubspot.com/marketing/goals-vs-objectives.

Frazzetto, Anna. "5 Mistakes Companies Make When Analyzing Customer Data—And How to Avoid Them." *CIO*. September 14, 2017. https://www.cio.com/article/3224571/5-mistakes-companies-make-when-analyzing-customer-data-and-how-to-avoid-them.html.

Gadiesh, Orit and James Gilbert. "How to Map Your Industry's Profit Pool." *Harvard Business Review*. May 1998. https://hbr.org/1998/05/how-to-map-your-industrys-profit-pool.

———. "Profit Pools: A Fresh Look at Strategy." *Harvard Business Review*. May 1998. https://hbr.org/1998/05/profit-pools-a-fresh-look-at-strategy.

Gal, David. "A Psychological Law of Inertia and the Illusion of Loss Aversion." *Judgment and Decision Making.* July 2006.

Ganti, Akhilesh. "Rational Choice Theory Definition." Investopedia. April 29, 2020. https://www.investopedia.com/terms/r/rational-choice-theory.asp.

Garton, Eric. "Is Your Company Actually Set Up to Support Your Strategy?" *Harvard Business Review*. November 22, 2017. https://hbr.org/2017/11/is-your-company-actually-set-up-to-support-your-strategy.

———. "Your Organization Wastes Time. Here's How to Fix It." *Harvard Business Review*. March 13, 2017. https://hbr.org/2017/03/your-organization-wastes-time-heres-how-to-fix-it.

Gecis, Zbignev. "8 Things to Use in 'Jobs-To-Be-Done' Framework for Product Development." UX Design. December 17, 2015. https://uxdesign.cc/8-things-to-use-in-jobs-to-be-done-framework-for-product-development-4ae7c6f3c30b.

Ghoshal, Sumantra. "Changing the Role of Top Management: Beyond Structure to Process." *Harvard Business Review*. January 1995. https://hbr.org/1995/01/changing-the-role-of-top-management-beyond-structure-to-processes.

Gibbs, Nicki. "Financial Marketers Must Align Purpose, Mission and Values Now." The Financial Brand. August 11, 2020. https://thefinancialbrand.com/98901/financial-marketers-purpose-mission-values-employee-retention-loyalty/.

Gino, Francesca and Bradley Staats. "Why Organizations Don't Learn." *Harvard Business Review.* November 2015. https://hbr.org/2015/11/why-organizations-dont-learn.

Gleeson, Brent. "How Important is Culture Fit for Employee Retention?" *Forbes.* April 3, 2017. https://www.forbes.com/sites/brentgleeson/2017/04/03/how-important-is-culture-fit-for-employee-retention/?sh=50b7f2477839.

Gorman, China. "Pump Up Your Change Management Competencies." ChinaGorman. September 30, 2014. https://chinagorman.com/2014/09/30/pump-up-your-change-management-competencies/.

Grabmeier, Jeff. "This Is Your Brain Detecting Patterns." ScienceDaily. May 31, 2018. https://www.sciencedaily.com/releases/2018/05/180531114642.htm.

Grace, David. "A Fundamental Human Flaw: Loyalty to the Tribe." Medium. November 1, 2018. https://medium.com/david-grace-columns-organized-by-topic/a-fundamental-human-flaw-loyalty-to-the-tribe-297afc1a95f0.

Graham, Paul. "How to Think for Yourself." PaulGraham. November 2020. http://paulgraham.com/think.html.

Graham, Shawn. "Understand What Your Customers Really Want." Deep Varnish. June 2017. https://deepvarnish.com/understanding-what-customers-value.

Grant, Adam. "Persuading the Unpersuadable." *Harvard Business Review.* March 2021. https://hbr.org/2021/03/persuading-the-unpersuadable.

Gray, Alex. "The 10 Skills You Need to Thrive in the Fourth Industrial Revolution." World Economic Forum. January 19, 2016. https://www.weforum.org/agenda/2016/01/the-10-skills-you-need-to-thrive-in-the-fourth-industrial-revolution/.

Grossman, David. "Why Context Is the Key to Employee Alignment." YourThoughtPartner. March 13, 2019. https://www.yourthoughtpartner.com/blog/bid/76561/why-context-is-king.

Gulati, Ranjay and James Olroyd. "The Quest for Customer Focus." *Harvard Business Review.* April 2005. https://hbr.org/2005/04/the-quest-for-customer-focus.

Guliati, Ranjay. "Silo Busting: How to Execute on the Promise of Customer Focus." *Harvard Business Review.* May 2007. https://hbr.org/2007/05/silo-busting-how-to-execute-on-the-promise-of-customer-focus.

Gupta, Sunil. "Are You Really Innovating around Your Customers' Needs?" *Harvard Business Review.* October 1, 2020. https://hbr.org/2020/10/are -you-really-innovating-around-your-customers-needs.

Gutnik, Lily. "The Role of Emotion in Decision Making." ScienceDirect. December 2006. https://www.sciencedirect.com/science/article/pii/ S1532046406000451.

Hagen, Paul. "The Rise of the Chief Customer Officer." *Harvard Business Review.* April 18, 2011. https://hbr.org/2011/04/the-rise-of-the-chief -customer.

Hall, Ericka. "Thinking in Triplicate." Medium. July 16, 2018. https://medium .com/mule-design/a-three-part-plan-to-save-the-world-98653a20a12f.

Harris, Michael. "Don't Let Metrics Undermine Your Business." *Harvard Business Review.* September 2019. https://hbr.org/2019/09/dont-let-metrics -undermine-your-business.

Harris, Michael. "When to Sell with Facts and Figures, and When to Appeal to Emotions." *Harvard Business Review.* January 26, 2015. https://hbr .org/2015/01/when-to-sell-with-facts-and-figures-and-when-to-appeal -to-emotions.

Harshadewa, Y. "Here's Why You Should Stop Using Personas." UX Collective. June 2, 2018. https://uxdesign.cc/heres-why-you-should-stop-using -personas-63c09a844e67.

Harvey, Steve. "How to Create a Differentiation Strategy." Fabrikbrands. March 10, 2021. https://fabrikbrands.com/how-to-create-a-differentiation -strategy/.

Haselton, M.G., Nettle, D., and Andrews, P.W. "The Evolution of Cognitive Bias." *The Handbook of Evolutionary Psychology.* Hoboken: John Wiley & Sons Inc., 2005.

Hastings, Reed. "Culture." Slideshare. 2001. https://www.slideshare.net /reed2001/culture-1798664/57-Increase_Talent_Density_Top_of.

Havice, Jennifer. "How to Create Customer Personas (with Actual, Real-Life Data)." CXL. April 21, 2019. https://cxl.com/blog/creating-customer -personas-using-data-driven-research/.

He, Yichen. "Designing for Enterprise vs. Designing for Consumers." UX Collective. December 10, 2020. https://uxdesign.cc/designing-for-enterprise -vs-designing-for-consumers-36a16f2281c2.

———. "What Does 'After UX' Even Mean?" UX Design. February 19, 2021. https://uxdesign.cc/what-does-after-ux-even-mean-7edc3d4febc4.

Healy, Mark. "The Three Problems with Customer Surveys." *Globe and Mail.* April 20, 2010. https://www.theglobeandmail.com/report-on-business /small-business/sb-marketing/the-three-problems-with-customer -surveys/article600084/.

Heick, Terry. "No, Your Brain Isn't Divided by Creativity and Logic." Teach-Thought. September 5, 2017. https://www.teachthought.com/learning/how-the-human-brain-works/.

Heid, Markham. "The Science Behind Gut Feelings." Medium. March 3, 2020. https://elemental.medium.com/the-science-behind-gut-feelings-e4ed0be994e9.

Heifetz, Ronald and Donald Laurie. "The Work of Leadership." *Harvard Business Review*. December 2001. https://hbr.org/2001/12/the-work-of-leadership?utm_source=linkedin&utm_campaign=hbr&utm_medium=social.

Heimans, Jeremy and Henry Timms. "Understanding 'New Power.'" *Harvard Business Review*. December 2014. https://hbr.org/2014/12/understanding-new-power?utm_medium=social&utm_source=linkedin&utm_campaign=hbr.

Herka, Iwo. "The Curse of Knowledge." Toward Data Science. November 16, 2019. https://towarddatascience.com/the-curse-of-knowledge-8deb4769bff9.

Hill, Andrea. "Confused about Jobs to be Done? So Was I." Medium. January 27, 2019. https://afhill.medium.com/confused-about-jobs-to-be-done-so-was-i-fa2ad70672ef.

Hinds, Pamela. "The Curse of Expertise: The Effects of Expertise and Debiasing Methods on Prediction of Novice Performance." *Journal of Experimental Psychology: Applied*. 1999.

Hirsch, Wendy. "Change Context: Why It Matters and How to Use It to Tailor Your Change Management Approach." WendyHirsch. February 7, 2019. https://wendyhirsch.com/blog/context-impact-on-change-management.

Holland, Kyle. "Eight Steps to Practical Problem Solving." Kaizen News. September 16, 2013. https://www.kaizen-news.com/eight-steps-practical-problem-solving/.

———. "The Gemba Walk." Industrial Lean. August 13, 2013. https://www.lean-news.com/the-gemba-walk/.

Hollander, S.C., Rassuli, K.M. Jones, G.D.B., and Dix, L.F. "Periodization in Marketing History." *Journal of Macromarketing*, Vol. 25 No. 1, June 2005.

Holliday, Ben. "Hypothesis in User Research and Discovery." Medium. March 10, 2019. http://webcache.googleusercontent.com/search?q=cache:3urUQpi2JEIJ:https://medium.com/leading-service-design/hypotheses-in-user-research-and-discovery-82b17577c7d&hl=en&gl=us&strip=1&vwsrc=0.

Holmes, Richard. "Product Monetization Plans." Department of Product. April 22, 2021. https://www.departmentofproduct.com/blog/product-monetization-strategies/.

Huang, Laura and Ryan Yu. "How to (Actually) Change Someone's Mind."
    Harvard Business Review. July 31, 2020. https://hbr.org/2020/07/how-to
    -actually-change-someones-mind.

Imber, Amantha. "Stop Asking for Feedback." *Harvard Business Review.*
    November 16, 2020. https://hbr-org.cdn.ampproject.org/c/s/hbr.org/amp
    /2020/11/stop-asking-for-feedback.

Jackson, Keith. "How to Make Decisions." Mindtools. February 3, 2021. https://
    www.mindtools.com/pages/article/newTED_00.htm.

Jimenez, Alex. "Digital Transformation Is About New Business Models, Not
    New Tech." The Financial Brand. March 23, 2021. https://thefinancial
    brand.com/110601/digital-transformation-is-about-new-business
    -models-not-new-tech/?edigest1.

Jin, Khong Lim. "Examining the Literature on Organizational Structure and
    Success." CFPS. February 5, 2021. https://www.cfps.org.sg/publications
    /the-college-mirror/article/1098.

Johnson, J. "Unpacking Trader Joe's." Harvard Business School. December
    9, 2015. https://digital.hbs.edu/platform-rctom/submission/unpacking
    -trader-joes/.

Joll, Katie. "Is It Time to Revisit Your Customer Personas." AudienceOps.
    June 18, 2020. https://webcache.googleusercontent.com/search?q=cache
    :5se7x0_drL8J:https://audienceops.com/time-revisit-customer-personas
    /+&cd=2&hl=en&ct=clnk&gl=us.

Jones, Stacey. "What Can the Brain Teach Us about Complex Problem Solv-
    ing?" Accenture Insights. January 19, 2019. https://www.accenture.com
    /nl-en/blogs/insights/what-can-the-brain-teach-us-about-complex
    -problem-solving.

Justo, AJ. "The Knowns and Unknowns Framework for Design Thinking."
    UX Design. February 17, 2019. https://uxdesign.cc/the-knowns-and
    -unknowns-framework-for-design-thinking-6537787de2c5.

Kahn, Saeed. "A Framework for Understanding Value." Medium. February
    4, 2020. https://swkhan.medium.com/a-framework-for-understanding
    -value-25a8eefcf61c.

Kahneman, Daniel and Ed Diener. *Well-Being: The Foundations of Hedonistic
    Psychology.* Sage, 2003.

Kahneman, Daniel, Knetsch, J.L., and Thaler, Richard. "Anomalies: The
    Endowment Effect, Loss Aversion, and Status Quo Bias." *The Journal of
    Economic Perspectives.* 1991.

Keener, Matt. "What are Different Types of Customer Data?" Insightly.
    April 16, 2020. https://www.insightly.com/blog/2020/04/customer-data
    -types/.

Kegan, Robert. "Immunity to Change." Schultz Consulting Group. March 2016. http://schultzcg.com/wp-content/uploads/2016/03/Immunity-to -Change.pdf.

Kenny, Graham. "Data Is Great—But It's Not a Replacement for Talking to Customers." *Harvard Business Review.* March 5, 2021. https://hbr.org/2021/03 /data-is-great-but-its-not-a-replacement-for-talking-to-customers.

———. "Put Your Metrics where Your Mouth Is." *Harvard Business Review.* October 2, 2020. https://hbr.org/2020/10/put-your-metrics-where-your -mouth-is.

Khawaja, Nick. "Dashboard vs Scorecard—Clarifying the Differences to Implement a Data Driven Performance Management System." LinkedIn. April 4, 2020. https://www.linkedin.com/pulse/dashboard-vs-scorecard -clarifying-differences-data-driven-khawaja/.

Kirch, Wilhelm. *Encyclopedia of Public Health.* Springer, 2008.

Klemet, Alan. "Know the Two—Very—Different Interpretations of Jobs to Be Done." JTBD. January 15, 2018. https://jtbd.info/know-the-two-very -different-interpretations-of-jobs-to-be-done-5a18b748bd89.

———. "What Is Jobs to be Done (JTBD)." JTBD. October 9, 2016. https://jtbd. info/2-what-is-jobs-to-be-done-jtbd-796b82081cca.

———. "Yes, Personas Focus on Demographics (and How to Fix That)." JTBD. June 21, 2018. https://jtbd.info/yes-personas-focus-on-demographics -and-how-to-fix-that-f27c02498e9d.

Kocina, Lonny. "What Percentage of New Products Fail and Why?" Publicity. May 3, 2017. https://www.publicity.com/marketsmart-newsletters /percentage-new-products-fail/.

Kreger, Alex. "5 Digital-First Strategies That Can Turn Banks into UX Disruptors." The Financial Brand. February 20, 2021. https://thefinancialbrand .com/102103/digital-first-design-strategies-banks-ux-disruptors -challenger-ecosystem/?edigest.

Kulbyte, Toma. "37 Customer Experience Statistics You Need to Know For 2021." Superoffice. January 4, 2021. https://www.superoffice.com/blog /customer-experience-statistics/.

Ladd, Brittain. "Ron Johnson Killed J. C. Penney—But He Has Become One of the Brightest Minds in Retail." *Observer.* June 10, 2019. https://observer .com/2019/06/ron-johnscon-jc-penney-retail-guru/.

Lalonde, Joseph. "Quotes and Leadership Lessons from Ford v Ferrari." JMLamonde. November 24, 2020. https://www.jmlalonde.com/quotes-and -leadership-lessons-from-ford-v-ferrari/.

Lange, Paul A. M. Van, Kruglanski, Arie W., and Higgins, E. Tory. *Handbook of Theories of Social Psychology: Collection: Volume 1 and 2.* Sage, 2011.

Lee K. and Kang, K.C. "Usage Context as Key Driver for Feature Selection." *SPLC*, vol. 6287 (2010). doi: 10.1007/978-3-642-15579-6.

Lee, Helena. "The Babies Who Nap in Sub-Zero Temperatures." *BBC News.* February 16, 2021. https://www.bbc.com/news/magazine-21537988.

Lee, Ju-Yeon. "Customer Centric Org Charts Aren't Right for Every Company." *Harvard Business Review.* July 2015. https://hbr.org/2015/06/customer -centric-org-charts-arent-right-for-every-company.

Legg, Timothy. "Is Cognitive Bias Affecting Your Decisions?" Healthline. May 28, 2020. https://www.healthline.com/health/mental-health/cognitive -bias#avoiding-it.

Leinwald, Paul and Cesare Mainardi. "The Coherence Premium." *Harvard Business Review.* June 2010. https://hbr.org/2010/06/the-coherence-premium.

Leinwand, Paul and Matthias Baumler. "8 Tough Question to Ask About Your Company's Strategy." *Harvard Business Review.* November 29, 2017. https://hbr.org/2017/11/8-tough-questions-to-ask-about-your-companys -strategy.

Leonard, David. "Most Change Initiatives Fail, but They Don't Have to." Gallup. May 24, 2013. https://news.gallup.com/businessjournal/162707 /change-initiatives-fail-don.aspx.

Leonard, Dorothy. "Spark Innovation through Empathic Design." *Harvard Business Review.* November 1997. https://hbr.org/1997/11/spark -innovation-through-empathic-design.

Leonard, Skip. "The Purpose of Action Learning." Learning thru Action. January 20, 2016. https://learningthruaction.com/the-purpose-of-action -learning/.

Liu, Ying. "The Challenges of Business Analytics: Successes and Failures." Hawaii International Conference on System Sciences. 2018. https://core .ac.uk/download/pdf/143480944.pdf.

Lucker, John and Trevor Bischoff. "Predictably Inaccurate: The Prevalence and Perils of Bad Big Data." Deloitte Insights. July 31, 2017. https://www2 .deloitte.com/us/en/insights/deloitte-review/issue-21/analytics-bad -data-quality.html.

Lutke, Tobi. "The Observer Effect." The Observer Effect. December 16, 2020. https://www.theobservereffect.org/tobi.html.

Markey, Rob. "Five Ways to Learn Nothing from Your Customer's Feedback." *Harvard Business Review.* December 9, 2013. https://hbr.org/2013/12/five -ways-to-learn-nothing-from-your-customers-feedback.

Marous, Jim. "It's Time to Throw Out Your 2020 Strategic Plan." The Financial Brand. August 19, 2020. https://thefinancialbrand.com/95243/digital -banking-strategic-business-plan-post-covid-19-coronavirus/?edigest.

Marquardt, Michael. "Harnessing the Power of Action Learning." WIAL. June 2004. https://wial.org/wp-content/uploads/Harnessing_the_Power_of _Action_Learning.pdf.

Marr, Bernard. "Five Signs Your Organization Is a Data Hoarder." Bernard Marr and Co. January 26, 2021. https://www.bernardmarr.com/default .asp?contentID=1370.

Mauboussin, Michael. "The True Measures of Success." *Harvard Business Review.* October 2012. https://hbr.org/2012/10/the-true-measures-of -success.

Mautz, Scott. "Elon Musk Completely Ignores Market Research. Here's When You Should Too." *INC.* February 10, 2021. https://www.inc.com/scott -mautz/elon-musk-completely-ignores-market-research-heres-when -you-should-too.html.

McAllister, Sonya. "Customers 2020: A Progress Report." Walker. August 2019. https://www.walkerinfo.com/knowledge-center/featured-research -reports/customers-2020-a-progress-report.

McCaffrey, Tony and Jim Pearson. "Find Innovation Where You Least Expect It." *Harvard Business Review.* December 2015. https://hbr.org/2015/12 /find-innovation-where-you-least-expect-it?referral=00060.

McCullough, Cathy. "Strategic Leadership vs. Tactical Leadership: Which Management Style Are You?" Rhythm Systems (blog). June 30, 2020. https://www.rhythmsystems.com/blog/strategic-vs.-tactical-leaders -which-are-you.

McFarland, Daniel. "Big Data and the Danger of Being Precisely Inaccurate." SagePub. 2015. https://journals.sagepub.com/doi/full/10.1177/205395171 5602495.

Miessler, Daniel. "Examples of Bad Metrics." DanielMiessler.com. May 27, 2019. https://danielmiessler.com/blog/how-to-create-bad-metrics-incentivize -wrong-behaviors/.

Miskinis, Julie. "Business Lessons from 'Ford v. Ferrari.'" *MIT Sloan Review.* January 7, 2020. https://news.mit.edu/2020/business-lessons-ford-v-ferrari -0107.

Mistry, Ravi. "The Future of Dashboards Is Dashboardless." Medium. February 19, 2021. https://scribblr42.medium.com/the-future-of-dashboards -is-dashboardless-6f746ea7d850.

Morgan, Blake. "The Case against a Chief Customer Officer." *Forbes.* January 5, 2020. https://webcache.googleusercontent.com/search?q=cache :7s5bOk2bSSwJ:https://www.forbes.com/sites/blakemorgan/2020/01 /05/the-case-against-a-chief-customer-officer/+&cd=1&hl=en&ct=clnk &gl=us.

Moss Kanter, Rosabeth. "Innovation: The Classic Traps." *Harvard Business Review*. November 2006. https://hbr.org/2006/11/innovation-the-classic-traps.

———. "Ten Reasons People Resist Change." *Harvard Business Review*. September 25, 2012. https://hbr.org/2012/09/ten-reasons-people-resist-chang.

Mourdoukoutas, Panos. "A Strategic Mistake That Haunts JC Penney." *Forbes*. September 27, 2013. https://webcache.googleusercontent .com/search?q=cache:G_6fjHcz2f0J:https://www.forbes.com/sites /panosmourdoukoutas/2013/09/27/a-strategic-mistake-that-haunts-j-c -penney/+&cd=4&hl=en&ct=clnk&gl=us.

Myer, Erin. "When Culture Doesn't Translate." *Harvard Business Review*. October 2015. https://hbr.org/2015/10/when-culture-doesnt-translate.

Natarelli, Mario. "How Emotion Drives Brand Choices and Decisions." Branding Strategy Insider. November 14, 2017. https://www .brandingstrategyinsider.com/how-emotion-drives-brand-choices-and -decisions/#.YJ_v2GZKhXR.

Nohria, Nitin. "Cracking the Code of Change." *Harvard Business Review*. May 2000. https://hbr.org/2000/05/cracking-the-code-of-change.

Omale, Gloria. "Gartner Says Nearly 90% of Organizations Now Have a Chief Experience Officer or Chief Customer Officer or Equivalent." Gartner. February 10, 2020. https://www.gartner.com/en/newsroom/press-releases /2020-02-10-gartner-says-nearly-90--of-organizations-now-have-a-c.

Oppong, Thomas. "If You Want to Persuade Someone, Start by Showing Them How They're Right." Ladders. September 19, 2019. https://www .theladders.com/career-advice/if-you-want-to-persuade-someone-start -by-showing-them-how-theyre-right.

———. "Psychologists Explain How Emotions, Not Logic Drive Human Behavior." Medium. January 3, 2019. https://medium.com/personal -growth/psychologists-explain-how-emotions-not-logic-drive-human -behaviour-6ed0daf76e1a.

P, Margaret. "Kill Your Personas." Medium. November 8, 2018. https:// medium.com/microsoft-design/kill-your-personas-1c332d4908cc.

Parker, Michael. "The Techniques I Use to Easily Turn User Testing into Actionable Insights." UX Collective. January 15, 2020. http://webcache .googleusercontent.com/search?q=cache:q9V1kQ1-qWgJ:https://uxdesign .cc/the-techniques-i-use-to-easily-turn-user-testing-into-actionable -insights-97d526267cd8&hl=en&gl=us&strip=1&vwsrc=0.

Pattillo, Ali. "The Power of Mindset: 4 Steps to Overcome Decision-Making Paralysis." Inverse. September 19, 2020. https://www.inverse.com/mind -body/power-of-mindsets-decision-paralysis.

Peppers, Don. "In Customer Relationships, Context Is King." *Fast Company.* August 27, 2012. https://www.fastcompany.com/3000758/customer -relationships-context-king.

Pereira, Hugo. "Using 'Truth Filtering' Process to Generate More Actionable Research." Medium. August 23, 2020. https://medium.com/truthfiltering /an-interactive-research-plan-template-that-leads-to-more-actionable -research-8e7434f7fe8e.

Perrey, Jesko and Dennis Spillecke. "How Marketers Can Avoid Big Data Blind Spots." *Harvard Business Review.* December 23, 2013. https://hbr.org/2013 /12/how-marketers-can-avoid-big-data-blind-spots.

Pfeil, John. "Why Jumping to Solutions Hurts Opportunity Exploration." Ideas to Go. February 6, 2019. https://www.ideastogo.com/articles-on -innovation/opportunity-discovery-and-jumping-to-solutions#:~:text =When%20two%20or%20more%20individuals,different%E2%80%94 and%20sub%2Doptimal%E2%80%94.

Pichler, Roman. "10 Tips for Using Key Performance Indicators." Roman-Pichler (blog). December 14, 2015. https://www.romanpichler.com/blog /10-tips-for-product-key-performance-indicators-kpis/.

Poon, Connie. "On the Psychology of Self-Prediction: Consideration of Situational Barriers to Intended Actions." *SJDM.* May 2014. http://journal.sjdm .org/14/14130/jdm14130.html.

Popov, Peio. "What Is the Data, Information, Knowledge, Wisdom (DIKW) Pyramid?" Ontotext. January 27, 2021. https://www.ontotext.com /knowledgehub/fundamentals/dikw-pyramid/.

Portigal, Steve. "Great User Research (for Non-Researchers)—Part 2." Medium. December 4, 2020. https://medium.com/user-research-explained/great -user-research-for-non-researchers-part-2-f8cae9f434a2.

Povey, Dean. "Why Roadmaps Fail." Medium. March 19, 2021. https://dean -povey.medium.com/why-feature-roadmaps-fail-3cac50fb8339.

Pupius, Dan. "Good Objective, Bad Objective." Range. January 22, 2019. https:// www.range.co/blog/good-objective-bad-objective.

Qonita, A. "Exploratory Design Research Interview." Medium. October 21, 2018. https://medium.com/designstrat/exploratory-design-research-interview -dc51398c6354.

Ransbotham, Sam. "Does Your Company Collect Data—or Hoard It?" *MIT Sloan Review.* July 28, 2014. https://sloanreview.mit.edu/article/does -your-company-collect-data-or-hoard-it/.

"Reg Revans." *Action Learning Associates.* 2021. https://www.actionlearning associates.co.uk/action-learning/reg-revans/

Reichardt, Frans. "What You Can Learn from Ryanair's Customer Centricity." FransReichardt.com. January 4, 2015. https://fransreichardt.com/what -you-can-learn-from-ryanairs-customer-centricity/.

Reichheld, Frederick. "The One Number You Need to Grow." *Harvard Business Review.* December 2003. https://hbr.org/2003/12/the-one-number -you-need-to-grow.

Revans, R.W. *ABC of Action Learning.* London: Lemos and Crane, 1998.

Ri, Sven. "How to Identify Customer Needs and Expectations." Userlike. September 27, 2016. https://www.userlike.com/en/blog/identify-customer -needs-expectations.

Rite, Sal. "How Stats Can Mislead You." Toward Data Science. November 23, 2018. https://towarddatascience.com/how-stats-can-mislead-you-e0ad5 63a578a.

Roberto, Michael. "Facing Ambiguous Threats." *Harvard Business Review.* November 2006. https://hbr.org/2006/11/facing-ambiguous-threats.

Roble, Greg. "What to do When Your Team Feels User Research Is Slowing Them Down." Medium. December 4, 2020. https://ggroble42.medium .com/what-to-do-when-your-team-feels-user-research-is-slowing -them-down-2d8467ec3dd3.

Roman, Christian. "The Problem with Personas. The Latest Debate Has Us Questioning . . ." Medium. February 26, 2019. https://medium.com /typecode/the-problem-with-personas-b6734a08d37a.

Rosen, Emanuel and Itamar Simonson. "How the Digital Age Rewrites the Rule Book on Consumer Behavior." Stanford Graduate School of Business. February 4, 2014. https://www.gsb.stanford.edu/insights/how -digital-age-rewrites-rule-book-consumer-behavior.

Rosen, Larry C. "Human Psychology Is Easy." Medium. February 15, 2020. http://webcache.googleusercontent.com/search?q=cache:WhGuPA195 _EJ:https://medium.com/better-humans/simple-mind-theory-55b8113 2640b&hl=en&gl=us&strip=1&vwsrc=0.

Rosenberg, Rebecca. "A Brief History of Customer Feedback." Hummsystems. December 10, 2019. https://www.hummsystems.com/posts/a-brief -history-of-customer-feedback.

Ross, Jeanne and Beath, Cynthia. "You May Not Need Big Data After All." *Harvard Business Review.* December 2013. https://hbr.org/2013/12/you-may -not-need-big-data-after-all.

Rowland, Christopher. "On the Reliability of Retrieval-Induced Forgetting." Frontiers. November 21, 2014. https://www.frontiersin.org/articles /10.3389/fpsyg.2014.01343/full.

Rowley, Jennifer. "The DIKW Model for Knowledge Management and Data Value Extraction." I-Scoop. January 28, 2021. https://www.i-scoop.eu/big -data-action-value-context/dikw-model/ .

Rust, Roland. "Rethinking Marketing." *Harvard Business Review*. January 2010. https://hbr.org/2010/01/rethinking-marketing.

Ryback, Ralph. "Why We Resist Change." *Psychology Today*. January 25, 2017. https://www.psychologytoday.com/us/blog/the-truisms-wellness/201701/why-we-resist-change.

Safdar, Khadeeja and Inti Pacheco. "The Dubious Management Fad Sweeping Corporate America." *Wall Street Journal*. May 15, 2019. https://www.wsj.com/articles/the-dubious-management-fad-sweeping-corporate-america-11557932084.

Sahni, Sumit. "Action Learning with Impact." *Harvard Business Review*. March 20, 2015. https://www.harvardbusiness.org/action-learning-with-impact/.

Salazar, Kim. "Why Personas Fail." NNGroup. January 28, 2018. https://www.nngroup.com/articles/why-personas-fail/.

Salminen, Joni. "Risks and Disadvantages of Using Personas." The Persona Blog. May 11, 2020. https://persona.qcri.org/blog/risks-and-disadvantages-of-using-personas/.

Samson, Julien. "Why Context Matters in Writing." The Writing Cooperative. June 28, 2017. https://writingcooperative.com/why-context-matters-in-writing-f52ad075c07a.

Santos, Joah. "Financial Marketers Must Toss Meaningless Vanity Metrics That Don't Sell." The Financial Brand. December 3, 2020. https://thefinancialbrand.com/104269/bank-credit-union-marketing-metrics-measurement-branding-purpose-trend/?edigest2.

Saviste, Maria. "3 Tricks from UX Research That Can Help You Have Better Conversations." Prototypr. February 10, 2020. https://blog.prototypr.io/3-tricks-from-ux-research-that-can-help-you-have-better-conversations-fe4c5a66379d.

Sawyer, Keith. *Group Genius*. New York: Perseus Books, 2007.

Schantz, John. "9 Proven Tips for Successful Change Management." Root Inc. October 5, 2017. https://www.rootinc.com/blog/successful-change-management-9-tips/.

Scholz, R.W. *Decision Making Under Uncertainty: Cognitive Decision Research, Social Interaction, Development and Epistemology*. Elsevier, 1983.

Schorin, Gerald and Mike Wilberding. "The X Factor of Great Corporate Cultures." *Harvard Business Review*. January 21, 2020. https://hbr.org/2020/01/the-x-factor-of-great-corporate-cultures.

Schrage, Michael. "Who Do You Want Your Customers to Become?" *Harvard Business Review*. July 17, 2012. https://hbr.org/2012/07/who-do-you-want-your-customers.

Schwager, Andre and Chris Meyer. "Understanding Customer Experience." *Harvard Business Review*. February 2007. https://hbr.org/2007/02/understanding-customer-experience.

Schwartz, Tony. "Leaders Focus Too Much on Changing Policies, Not Enough on Change." *Harvard Business Review*. June 25, 2018. https://hbr.org/2018/06/leaders-focus-too-much-on-changing-policies-and-not-enough-on-changing-minds.

Scott, Anthony. "Turning Customer Intelligence into Innovation." *Harvard Business Review*. August 20, 2012. https://hbr.org/2012/08/turning-customer-intelligence.

Selden, Larry. "Manage Customer-Centric Innovation—Systematically." *Harvard Business Review*. April 2006. https://hbr.org/2006/04/manage-customer-centric-innovation-systematically.

Sg, Kritanya. "Do We Always Know What Our Users Really Need?" UX Collective. October 21, 2020. https://uxdesign.cc/do-we-always-know-what-our-users-want-678ccf058965.

Shabaugh, Rebecca. "How to Unlock Your Team's Creativity." *Harvard Business Review*. January 21, 2019. https://hbr.org/2019/01/how-to-unlock-your-teams-creativity.

Shapiro, Ellen. "Is Design Thinking Really BS?" Medium. January 4, 2020. http://webcache.googleusercontent.com/search?q=cache:E5T3779vy-oJ:https://uxdesign.cc/is-design-thinking-really-bs-5deb6c333f2&hl=en&gl=us&strip=1&vwsrc=0.

Shaw, Ben. "Puncturing the Paradox: Group Cohesion and the Generational Myth." BBH Labs. May 8, 2020. http://bbh-labs.com/puncturing-the-paradox-group-cohesion-and-the-generational-myth/.

Shaw, Colin. "The 5 Rules of Behavioral Journey Mapping." CXPA. August 14, 2020. https://www.cxpa.org/blogs/colin-shaw/2020/08/14/the-5-rules-of-behavioral-journey-mapping.

Shaw, Robert. "So You Think You Understand Revenues." *Harvard Business Review*. May 2007. https://hbr.org/2007/05/so-you-think-you-understand-revenues.

Shestopalov, Slava. "Feature Prioritizing: 3 Ways to Reduce Subjectivity and Bias." UX Collective. December 23, 2020. https://uxdesign.cc/feature-prioritization-a089fd0af08.

Silverthorne, Sean. "When Goal Setting Goes Bad." *Harvard Business School Working Knowledge*. March 2, 2009. https://hbswk.hbs.edu/item/when-goal-setting-goes-bad.

Skrobe, Robert. "A Simplified Approach to Design Spring Problem Framing." Medium. February 11, 2019. https://medium.com/dallas-design-sprints/a-simplified-approach-to-design-sprint-problem-framing-65d3bf271693.

Smith, A.C. "Action Learning: Worth a Closer Look." *Ivey Business Quarterly*. September 1997. http://www.tlainc.com/ifalcivy.htm.

Smith, Quincy. "6 Of My Favorite Case Studies in Data Science." Big Data Made Simple. December 6, 2018. https://bigdata-madesimple.com/6-of-my -favorite-case-studies-in-data-science/.

Southerton, D. *Encyclopedia of Consumer Culture.* Thousand Oaks: Sage, 2011.

Speicher, Max. "KPI Centered Design." UX Collective. March 13, 2020. http:// webcache.googleusercontent.com/search?q=cache:HpovQORVuq8J :https://uxdesign.cc/kpi-centered-design-8d1f4e231a5&hl=en&gl =us&strip=1&vwsrc=0.

Spool, Jared. "Jobs to Be Done: An Occasionally Useful UX Gimmick." UIE. January 17, 2019. https://articles.uie.com/jobs-to-be-done-an-occasionally -useful-ux-gimmick/.

———. "Making Personas Useful by Making Them Scenario-Based." UIE. June 19, 2019. https://articles.uie.com/making-personas-truly-valuable -by-making-them-scenario-based/.

———. "When it Comes to Personas, the Real Value Is in the Scenarios." Medium. September 18, 2018. https://medium.com/user-interface-22/when -it-comes-to-personas-the-real-value-is-in-the-scenarios-4405722dd55c.

Spradlin, Dwayne. "Are You Solving the Right Problem?" *Harvard Business Review.* September 2012. https://hbr.org/2012/09/are-you-solving-the -right-problem.

Springman, Jack. "Six Reasons Why Customer-Centricity Should Not Be an Objective." MyCustomer. March 9, 2020. https://www.mycustomer .com/customer-experience/engagement/six-reasons-why-customer -centricity-should-not-be-an-objective.

Sterling, Christa. "What Happens to Your Brain When You Learn a New Skill?" CCSU. July 25, 2017. https://ccsuconed.wordpress.com/2017/07/25 /what-happens-to-your-brain-when-you-learn-a-new-skill/.

Streeter, Bill. "A Hybrid Fintech Startup Foretells Banking's Future." The Financial Brand. June 29, 2020. https://thefinancialbrand.com/97502/ hybrid-fintech-startup-challenger-bank-credit-maketplace-platform /?edigest.

Struck, Brooke. "Why Do We Focus on Items or Information That Are More Prominent and Ignore Those That Are Not?" The Decision Lab. January 4, 2021. https://thedecisionlab.com/biases/salience-bias/.

Su, Pacs. "Lessons in Building a Culture of Collabotonomy in Product Design." Medium. January 26, 2019. https://medium.com/ro-design /lessons-in-building-a-culture-of-collabotonomy-in-product-design -18c26de9d63b.

Sullivan, Bob. "Know Your Nuggets: The Google Effect." PeopleScience. Feburary 4, 2020. https://peoplescience.maritz.com/Articles/2020/Know-Your -Nuggets-The-Google-Effect.

Sznel, Monika. "Your Next Persona Will Be Non-Human—Tools for Envi-
    ronment-Centered Designers." UX Design. September 12, 2020.
    https://uxdesign.cc/your-next-persona-will-be-non-human-tools-for
    -environment-centered-designers-c7ff96dc2b17.
Tasler, Nick. "Stop Using the Excuse 'Organizational Change Is Hard.'" Har-
    vard Business Review. July 19, 2017. https://hbr.org/2017/07/stop-using-the
    -excuse-organizational-change-is-hard.
Taylor, Bill. "Don't Let Negativity Sink Your Organization." Harvard Business
    Review. February 17, 2020. https://hbr.org/2020/02/dont-let-negativity
    -sink-your-organization.
Tedlow, R.A. and Jones, G. The Rise and Fall of Mass Marketing. Routledge, 1993.
Thaler, Richard and Cass Sunstein. Nudge: Improving Decisions About Health,
    Wealth, and Happiness. Penguin, 2008.
Thomadsen, Raphael. "How Context Affects Choice." SpringerLink. November
    25, 2017. https://link.springer.com/article/10.1007/s40547-017-0084-9.
Thompson, S.C. "Illusions of Control: How We Overestimate Our Personal
    Influence." Current Directions in Psychological Science. 1999.
Tollman, Peter and Andrew Toma. "A New Approach to Organization Design."
    Boston Consulting Group. April 5, 2016. https://www.bcg.com/publications
    /2016/people-organization-new-approach-organization-design.
Torre, Jose. "The Design Process Is a Lie." Shopify UX. January 6, 2021. http://
    webcache.googleusercontent.com/search?q=cache:GKABsopMXF0J
    :https://ux.shopify.com/the-design-process-is-a-lie-465a7064a733&hl=e
    n&gl=us&strip=1&vwsrc=0.
Turner, DM. "The Value of Storytelling in Organizational Change." Turner
    Change Management, Inc. 2015. https://thinktransition.com/the-value
    -of-storytelling-in-organizational-change/.
Turner, Luke. "Action Learning—Overview, Guide, Example of How It Works."
    Corporate Finance Institute. 2017. https://corporatefinanceinstitute.com
    /resources/knowledge/other/action-learning/.
Turner, Neil. "This MVP Madness Must Stop." UX Collective. November 30,
    2020. https://uxdesign.cc/this-mvp-madness-must-stop-ee05d65e553e.
Tversky, Amos and Daniel Kahneman. "Judgment under Uncertainty: Heuris-
    tics and Biases." Science. September 1974.
Ulwick, Tony. "Avoid These Common Mistakes When Getting Started with
    Jobs-To-Be-Done." JobsToBeDone. August 27, 2018. https://jobs-to-be
    -done.com/avoid-these-common-mistakes-when-getting-started-with
    -jobs-to-be-done-bd55ec91fcb2.
———. "Jobs to Be Done Framework." Strategyn. September 25, 2020. https://
    strategyn.com/jobs-to-be-done/customer-centered-innovation-map/.

Umbach, Heath. "6 Reasons Product Leaders Don't Talk to Customers." Medium. November 12, 2018. https://medium.com/@heathumbach/6-reasons-product-leaders-dont-talk-to-customers-b3627f74c2d6.

Van Opzeeland, Pascal. "8 Causes of Miscommunication and Misunderstanding." Userlike. July 13, 2017. https://www.userlike.com/en/blog/causes-of-miscommunication.

Vanderkam, Laura. "The First Question to Ask when You Sit Down to Work." Medium. January 11, 2020. https://forge.medium.com/the-first-question-to-ask-yourself-when-you-sit-down-to-work-69366165d8a.

Vaughan, Mike. "How to Ask Better Questions." TEDxMileHigh. TEDx Talks. Posted July 17, 2015. YouTube video. https://www.youtube.com/watch?v=J8xfuCcXZu8.

Verdoy, Alvaro. "The 10 Responsibilities of Marketing Departments." SaleSlayer (blog). December 23, 2013. https://blog.saleslayer.com/10-responsibilities-marketing-departments.

Vigen, Tyler. "Spurious Correlations." TylerVigen.com. January 26, 2021. http://www.tylervigen.com/spurious-correlations.

Vogiazou, Yanna. "Hacking the Design Sprint Method to Solve a Complex Problem." Medium. January 22, 2019. https://medium.com/nacar-design/hacking-the-design-sprint-method-1f00127aaabb.

Voyer, Eric. "Top 5 Examples of Market Research Failures." Traqline. September 14, 2016. https://www.traqline.com/newsroom/blog/top-5-examples-market-research-failure/.

Wang, Tricia. "The Human Insights Missing from Big Data." TED.com. September 2016. https://www.ted.com/talks/tricia_wang_the_human_insights_missing_from_big_data?language=en.

Warlop, Luk. "The Role of Usage Context in Consumer Choice: A Problem-Solving Perspective." ACR. 1993. https://www.acrwebsite.org/volumes/7478/volumes/v20/NA-20.

Warner, Sofia. "Trader Joe's—Technology and Operations Management." *Harvard Business School.* December 9, 2015. https://digital.hbs.edu/platform-rctom/submission/trader-joes/.

Warren, Todd. "Getting The Most of 'Getting Out Of The Building.'" *Forbes.* January 28, 2013.

Wedell-Wellsborg, Thomas. "Are You Solving the Right Problems?" *Harvard Business Review.* February 2017. https://hbr.org/2017/01/are-you-solving-the-right-problems.

Weinstein, Brian. "Moving Beyond the Net Promoter Score." Medium. June 24, 2018. https://bweinstein.medium.com/moving-beyond-the-net-promoter-score-9b560f3767ba.

Wellington, Elizabeth. "The Psychology Behind the Perfect Customer Inter-view." HelpScout. March 1, 2020. https://www.helpscout.com/blog/customer-interview/.

Wheeler, Marc. "Scrap the User Persona. Replace It with the Storyboard." Inside Design. July 24, 2019. https://www.invisionapp.com/inside-design/user-journey-storyboards/.

White, Duane. "Employee First Culture Risks Becoming Internally Focused and Externally Irrelevant." Aveus. 2020. https://aveus.com/employee-first-culture-risks-becoming-internally-focused-externally-irrelevant/.

Wilson, Fred. "Top 10 Problem Solving Activities for Your Team to Master." NTask. February 17, 2021. https://www.ntaskmanager.com/blog/top-problem-solving-activities-for-your-team-to-master/.

Wong, Robin. "Forget Elevator Pitches—Try a Safe Landing Instead." Medium. November 13, 2020. https://robinow.medium.com/forget-elevator-pitches-try-a-safe-landing-instead-f9c26eb8c9ea.

Yip, George. "Good Leadership Hinges on Organizational Intelligence." *Harvard Business Review.* June 15, 2020. https://hbr.org/2020/06/good-leadership-hinges-on-organizational-intelligence?utm_medium=social&utm_campaign=hbr&utm_source=linkedin.

Yohn, Denise Lee. "6 Ways to Build a Customer-Centric Culture." *Harvard Business Review.* October 2, 2018. https://hbr.org/2018/10/6-ways-to-build-a-customer-centric-culture.

———. "Six Surprising Facts That Explain Trader Joe's Secrets to Success." *Forbes.* June 13, 2018. https://www.forbes.com/sites/deniselyohn/2018/06/13/six-surprising-facts-that-explain-trader-joes-secrets-to-success/#1f6f69c21601.

Zak, Paul. "The Neuroscience of Trust." *Harvard Business Review.* February 2017. https://hbr.org/2017/01/the-neuroscience-of-trust.

Zealley, John and Robert Wollan. "Marketers Need to Stop Focusing on Loyalty and Start Thinking About Relevance." *Harvard Business Review.* March 21, 2018. https://hbr.org/2018/03/marketers-need-to-stop-focusing-on-loyalty-and-start-thinking-about-relevance.

Zhexembayeva, Nadya. "3 Things You're Getting Wrong About Organizational Change." *Harvard Business Review.* June 9, 2020. https://hbr.org/2020/06/3-things-youre-getting-wrong-about-organizational-change.

Zook, Chris and James Allen. "The Great Repeatable Business Model." *Harvard Business Review.* November 2011. https://hbr.org/2011/11/the-great-repeatable-business-model.

INDEX

A

abandonment, 8
accountability, 132. *See also* measurement
action. *See also* monetization strategy
translating concept into, 63
translating data into, 41–42
action learning, 89–94
advertisements, online, 64
affinity, unconscious, 50–51
airline accidents, 49
alignment, culture-strategy, 76–77, 79–80, 82, 85
Amazon, 66–67
American Express, 99–100
amygdala, 19n
ancillary revenue, 126
Apple, xii, 56, 57, 58, 59
archetypes, 51. *See also* customer personas
Arena swimwear, 84
assumptions, 32, 50, 103
attrition, 45. *See also* retention
autonomy, 79

B

Bain and Company, 71

Bane, Dan, 77, 78
Beethoven, Ludwig van, 145
behavioral economics, 20
behaviors, 70–72
changing, 74
counterproductive, 29
influences on, 110–111
judging others', 52
metrics' impact on, 140–141
organizational structures and, 71–72
priorities reflected in, 76
beliefs, existing, 51
bias, 20, 102. *See also* heuristics
bikeshedding, 25, 102
context effect, 26
curse of knowledge, 21–22, 102
in data, 39
Google effect, 26–27
interviews and, 103
in JTBD theory, 12–13
Maslow's hammer, 23–24, 30
need to consider, 30
past experiences and, 96
perceptual salience, 27–28, 60
plan continuation error, 49
status quo bias, 22–23
surrogation, 28–29, 140–141

bias (*continued*)
  in surveys, 97
  survivorship bias, 12–13
Big Data, 37, 78, 93
bikeshedding, 25, 102
binge watching, 44
Blank, Steve, 11n, 100
Boeing, 90–91
borrowing, 99
brain, 19
brand/revenue impact, 95–96
business acumen, 91

C
caring, 69
causation, vs. correlation, 38
CCO (chief customer officer),
  66–68
certainty, xiii
Challenger disaster, 47–49
change, 42. *See also* innovation
  creating and driving, 143
  resistance to, 23, 50, 147
character, judging others', 52, 55
chief customer officer (CCO),
  66–68
Christensen, Clayton, 11
CMO Council, 63
cognitive biases. *See* bias
Columbia Records, 68
comfort zones, 50
commentary, open, 53
commercialization, 129. *See also*
  monetization strategy
commitment, 43
Commonwealth Bank, 132
communications, xiii
company ancillary revenue, 126
company partnership revenue, 126
Competing Against Luck
  (Christensen), 11
competitors, 123

conditions, changing, 49
Confucius, 90
connections, 4. *See also* customer
  centricity
conservatism, 51–52. *See also*
  familiar; status quo
context, xiii, 3, 41, 45, 92–93, 98,
  137. *See also* drivers; "why"
context effect, 26
contrasts, 28
conversations, benefits of, 98
Cooper, Alan, 9
correlations, 37–38, 44n
cost
  of data collection, 95–96
  vs. revenue, 120
COVID-19 pandemic, 23
credit cards, 99–100
CRM (customer relationship
  management), 4
culture, company, 75–85
  alignment with business
    strategy, 75, 76–77, 79–80,
    82, 85
  change in, 81–83
  effectiveness, 75
  employee-first, 81
  inward- vs. outward-facing, 76
curse of knowledge, 21–22, 102
customer acquisition cost (CAC),
  4n
customer centricity, 4, 63, 64–65,
  66
customer communication tools, 4
customer data. *See* customer
  exploration; data; data
  collection; feedback; insight
customer direct revenue, 125–126
Customer Discovery, 100
customer engagement, 6, 7, 84, 97
customer experience, as
  differentiator, 8

customer experience leader, 66–68
customer exploration. *See also* data
    collection; feedback; insight
    changing objective of, 16
    in job descriptions, 84
    negative perception of, 13–14
customer feedback. *See* data
    collection; feedback; insight
customer indirect revenue, 126
customer journey, 5, 7–9
customer knowledge, 14–15, 16. *See
    also* customer exploration;
    data collection; feedback;
    insight
Customer Listener, The (blog), 65
customer mission, 73–74
customer personas, 5, 9–11, 51
customer relationship
    history of, 3–4
    ownership of, 66–68
customer relationship
    management (CRM), 4
customer retention, 4n, 124
customer satisfaction
    focus on, 4
    NPS, 5–7
customers
    gap with, 83
    ignoring, 58
    perspective of. *see* context;
        Query
    talking with, 8, 11n, 98
    understanding, 2
customers, new, 4, 119, 124. *See also*
    monetization strategy

D
Damasio, Antonio, 19
D'Amico, Mario, xiv–xv
dashboards, 139–140
data
    bias in, 39

Big Data, 37, 78, 93
    devices recording, 37
    vs. information, 38–39
    vs. knowledge, 44–45
    qualitative, xiv, 11, 139
    superficial, xiii
    translating into action, 41–42
    using, 5–13, 36–37, 43. *see also*
        methodologies
data collection, 4–5. *See also*
    customer exploration;
    feedback; insight
    changing, 16, 35
    charging all employees with,
        83–85
    as focus, 36
    purpose of, 2
    technology for, 4–5
data hoarding, 35–36
debt, 99
decisions, 37, 115–116
    Diversified Voting, 116
    autonomy to make, 79
    Challenger disaster and, 47–49
    difficulties of, 17–18
    emotion and, 18, 19, 20
    HIPPO power and, 145
    measurement and, 133
    mindsets and, 50
    rational thinking and, 20
Deloitte, 93
Delphi technique, 32–33
Deming, W. Edward, 69
detractors, 6, 7
Di Fiore, Alessandro, 84
differentiator, 8, 80, 104, 112
digital amnesia, 27n
direct revenue, 125–126
distractions, 88
Diversified Voting, 116
diversity, 51n
D'O, 84

door-to-door sales, 3
drivers, 135, 136, 138–139. *See also* context; "why"
Drucker, Peter, 69, 131

E
education, 88–93
effectiveness, 95–96
Einstein, Albert, 41, 88, 89, 132
Ellenberg, Jordan, 12
emotion, 18, 19, 20
employee-first culture, 81. *See also* culture, company
employees, 83–85. *See also* culture, company; organization
engagement, customer, 6, 7, 84, 97
engagement, employee, 81. *See also* culture, company
entrepreneurship, 100
environmental factors. *See* context
equity, 51n
errors, unconscious, 20. *See also* bias
Estimate-Talk-Estimate method, 32n
execution, 95–96
expectations, 65, 96. *See also* bias
Expedia, 60–61
experience, customer, 8
experience, past, 32
  expectations and, 96
  fixation on inefficient solution and, 61
experts, xvi
exploration, customer. *See* customer exploration; data collection; feedback; insight

F
familiar, 51–52, 58, 117. *See also* status quo
Fastenal, 73–74

feedback. *See also* customer exploration; data collection; insight
  barriers to, xv
  certainty and, xiii
  converting into new revenue streams, 119. *see also* monetization strategy
  effectively responding to, 79
  qualitative, xiv
  quantity of, 110
  reasons for not getting, 95–96
  reliability of, 116
  usefulness of, 116
  views of, xii
feedback capture. *See* customer exploration; data collection
financial department, 129
financials, 123
Flovik, Vegard, 38n
Ford, Henry, 24
Ford Motor Company, 98–99, 100
formulas, 56–58
frame of reference, 30
fundamental attribution error, 52

G
Gartner, 66
Gemba Walk, 92
Genchi Genbutsu, 92n
Geneen, Harold, 41–42
generalities, based on mindsets, 50
get-keep-grow objective, 123–124
Global Leadership Action Learning Program, 90–91
goals, 39–41
Godin, Seth, 119
Goodhart's law, 29
Google effect, 26–27
Google searches, blamed for attrition, 45

Grant, Adam, 145n
groupthink, 104. *See also* mindsets
growth, 8, 39, 80, 122. *See also*
    monetization strategy

H
Haid, Jonathan, 20
hammer, 23–24
happiness, employee, 81. *See also*
    culture, company
Harvard Business Review, 84
Haydn, Josef, 145
helpfulness, 147
heuristics, 21n, 50. *See also* bias
    conservatism, 51–52
    effects of, 55–56
    fundamental attribution error,
        52
    intuition, 54, 59
    mindsets and, 50–54
    self-confirmation, 51, 57
    tribal loyalty, 53–54
    unconscious affinity, 50–51
Hidden Risk of AI and Big Data, The
    (Flovik), 38n
hierarchical organization, 69–70
HIPPO power, 145
hoarding, data, 35–36
Hobson, Jim, 55
"how", defining, 40–41
Hsieh, Tony, 63, 75
hypotheses, 100. *See also* Wow
    hypothesis

I
IBM, 41
implementation, 119, 123. *See also*
    monetization strategy
inclusion, 51n
indifference, customer, 6
indirect revenue, 126
inductive reasoning, 31, 32

Industrial Revolution, 3
influences, 145
information, 37
    vs. data, 38–39
    forgetting, 27
    translating into action, 41–42
information accessibility, 2
information apathy, 14
information overload, 20. *See also*
    bias
initiative performance, tracking,
    139
innovation, 11. *See also* change
    converting into profit, 120. *see*
        also monetization strategy
    resistance to, 117
insight, 37, 41. *See also* customer
    exploration; data collection;
    feedback
    access to, 68
    effectiveness of, 43
    need for, 16
instincts, 59
intent, xiii
interaction, customer, 79, 97
interaction, human, 77
internet, 26–27, 45
interviews, 2
    bias and, 103
    challenges of, 101–103
    verifying Wow hypothesis with,
        110–112, 114–115. *see also*
        3W Ideation process
Intuit, 84
intuition, 54, 59
iPhone, 29–30. *See also*
    smartphones

J
JCPenney, 56–58, 59
job descriptions, 84
Jobs, Steve, xii

Jobs to Be Done: Theory to Practice
      (Ulwick), 11
jobs-to-be-done theory (JTBD), 5,
      11–13
Johnson, Ron, 56–59
Johnson Instruments, 130
journey bias, 9
JTBD (jobs-to-be-done theory), 5,
      11–13
junk mail, 64

K
Kahneman, Daniel, 20, 55
Kelly, John, 41
Kennedy Space Center (KSC),
      47–48
key performance indicators (KPIs),
      132–133, 135
Khawaja, Nick, 140
knowing, 69
knowledge, 37, 41
      vs. data, 44–45
      fixation on inefficient solution
            and, 61
      vs. wisdom, 89
knowledge, curse of, 21–22, 102
knowledge, customer, 14–15, 16. *See
      also* data collection; feedback;
      insight
KPIs (key performance indicators),
      132–133, 135

L
laziness, mental, 53. *See also*
      heuristics
leaders, motivation of, 13
leadership skills, 91
Lean Launchpad, 100
Lean Startup, 100
learning, 88–94
Lexus, 93
logic, 20–21

Lund, Robert, 48
Lyautey, Hubert, 43

M
Managing (Geneen), 41–42
market research, 4
marketing era, 4
marketing team, 67
Marshall Space Flight Center
      (MSFC), 47–48
Maslow, Abraham, 24
Maslow's hammer, 23–24, 30
Maso, Jerry, 48
meaning, 37, 41–42
measurement, 131–141
      building architecture for,
            137–138
      choosing what to measure,
            132–134
      fixation on, xiii
      replacing objectives with
            metrics, 140–141
      scorecards, 138–140
      selecting right objectives for,
            135
      shifting, 134
      targets and, 29
      tracking individual initiative
            performance, 139
      vanity metrics, 134n
Medicare, 130
mental shortcuts, 50. *See also* bias;
      heuristics
messaging, 123
methodologies
      customer journey, 5, 7–9
      customer personas, 5, 9–11, 51
      JTBD, 5, 11–13
      net promoter score (NPS), 5–7,
            64
metrics, 134n, 140–141. *See also*
      measurement

Microsoft, 27, 52
Millennials, 99, 100
mimicry, 147
mindsets, 50, 147
    Challenger disaster and, 48
    generalities based on, 50
    heuristics and, 50–54
    open, 61
    reframing, 59–61
    shifting, 103. *see also* 3W
        Ideation process
    "Why Data Doesn't Change
        Minds", 50n
misalignment, 76–77, 82, 131, 132
mission, customer, 73–74
mission statement, 72–74
monetization leader, 128
monetization strategy, 119, 122. *See
    also* profit
    creating, 122–127
    establishing monetization
        leader, 128
    establishing viability, 122–123
    financial department and, 129
    get-keep-grow objective,
        123–124
    pricing and, 127–128
    revenue opportunity grid,
        124–127
MortonThiokol Inc. (MTI), 47–48
Musk, Elon, 58

N
NASA, 49
National Science Foundation
    Innovation Corps (NSF
    I-Corps), 100
Nature Neuroscience, 54
needs, 15
    future, 31
    hidden, 3, 103–104, 121. *see also*
        3W Ideation process

    source of, 3
net promoter score (NPS), 5–7, 64
Netflix, 44
noise, 145
Nokia, 52
Novartis, 91
NPS (net promoter score), 5–7, 64
numbers. *See* data

O
objectives, 70–71
    creating customer strategy
        scorecard and, 138–139
    defining, 39
    determining drivers of, 135
    in goals, 39–40
    replacing with metrics, 140–141
    targets and, 29
    value-added, 135–137
objectivity, 19
observations, benefits of, 98
Observer, The, 56
OFC (operation field counselors),
    43
Ogilvy, 9
Olam International, 71
Oldani, Davide, 84
O'Neill, Ryan, 60
online courses, 89
operation field counselors (OFC),
    43
opportunity, 87, 117
organization. *See also* employees
    resistance to change in, 50
    responsibility for customer
        relationship in, 66–68
organizational purpose, 72
organizational structure, 69–70
    behaviors and, 71–72
    employee-customer gap and, 83
    framework for, 70. *see also*
        principles

outcome-driven innovation, 11
outcomes
    focus on, 66
    improving, 133

P
pandemic, 23
partnership revenue, 126
passives, 6
path of least resistance, 27
patterns, 37–38
people, understanding, 2, 69
perceptions
    clarifying, 112
    influences on, 110–111
perceptual salience, 27–28, 60
performance, 131, 133. *See also*
    measurement
personas, customer, 5, 9–11, 51
perspectives. *See also* mindsets
    alternative, minimizing, 53–54
    customers', 106. *see also* context;
        Query
plan continuation error, 49
possibilities, multiple, 32
power
    HIPPO, 145
    reporting relationships and, 71
practicality, 19
practices, 71. *See also* behaviors
prediction, 31, 32
preference, 31, 53
price, 66, 127–128, 130
PricewaterhouseCoopers, 8
principles, 70–72. *See also*
    behaviors
priorities, reflected in behaviors,
    76–77
problem statement, 40n
problems, hidden, 84
problems, organizational
    defining, 40–41

reframing, 61
    solving, 88–94
process. *See also* 3W Ideation
    process
    negative perception of, 13
    observation of, 92–93
Procter & Gamble, 59
production era, 3
productivity
    emphasis on, 87
    employee engagement and,
        81
    wasted time, 88
products, as source of need, 3
profit. *See also* monetization
    strategy; revenue
    converting innovation into,
        120
    employee engagement and, 81
    finding sources of, 121–122
profit metrics, 132
promoters, 6–7
purchase behavior, 53
purpose, 37
purpose, organizational, 72

Q
qualitative data, xiv, 11, 139
Query, 105–106, 108, 109, 113. *See*
    also 3W Ideation process
questioning, 141–143
questionnaires, 2
questions, 101–103. *See also*
    interviews; surveys

R
radio technology, 117
ratings, motivation behind, 7. *See*
    also context
rationality, 19, 20
Rosser Reeves fallacy, xiii*n*
Reichardt, Frans, 65

relationship era, 4. *See also* customer centricity; customer relationship

reporting relationships, 71. *See also* organizational structure

research. *See also* customer exploration; data collection; insight

human-centered, 98

negative perception of, 13–14

responsibility for customer relationship, 66–68. *See also* organizational structure

retention, customer, 4n, 124

Revans, Reg, 89–92

revenue, 119–121, 125. *See also* monetization strategy; profit

revenue opportunity grid, creating, 124–127

review and discussion, 32–33

Righteous Mind, The (Haid), 20

Rio Tinto, 131–132

Rogers Commission, 48

Rubin, Rick, 68–69

Ryanair, 65–66

S

Salary.com, 88

sales era, 3

sales team, 67

Sandy (hurricane), 39

Sarnoff, David, 117

saturation point, 110

scandals, 37

Schneier, Bruce, 36

scorecard, 138–139

self-confirmation, 51, 57

serial killers, 55

service, value-added, 126–127

7-Eleven Japan, 43

shareholders, 80, 145

shortcuts, mental. *See* heuristics

Siemens, 91

similarities, 50–51

simple trade era, 3

Sloan, Matt, 78

smartphones, 29–30, 52

social media, 39

solution jumping, 91–93

Sony Walkman, xi–xii

spam, 64

specificity, 63, 70

spending, 99

Spurious Correlations (Vigen), 38

stakeholders, 131–132

start-ups, 100

statistics, 38

status quo, 22–23, 117. *See also* familiar

stereotypes, 51

storytelling exercises, customer-focused, 98

structure, organizational. *See* organizational structure

Sun Tzu, 35, 87, 131

sunk-cost fallacy, 49n

surrogation, 28–29, 140–141

surveys, 2

bias in, 97

pros and cons of, 96–97

survivorship bias, 12–13

Sutcliffe, Peter, 55

Swiffer, 59

T

Target, 56, 57

target audiences, understanding, 9, 10. *See also* customer personas

targets, measurement and, 29

TEDx talk, 50n

Tesla, xii, 58

theories, 100. *See also* Wow hypothesis

thinking, 90, 141–143

Thinking, Fast and Slow
    (Kahneman), 20
Thompson, Hunter S., 146
3W Ideation process, 104–117, 121n,
    122, 137
    Diversified Voting, 116
    interviews in, 110–112, 114–115
    in practice, 112–115
    preparing for, 115–116
    Query, 105–106, 108, 109, 113
    reliability in, 116
    usefulness in, 116
    "what", 104, 107–108, 109,
        113–114
    "why", 104, 106–107, 108, 109,
        113
    Wow hypothesis, 104, 108–112,
        114–115, 122
time, 87, 88
Torrey Canyon oil spill, 49
Toyota, 93
Trader Joe's, 77–80
training software, 89
tribal loyalty, 53–54

U
U-Haul, 121
UI (user interface design), 9n
Ulwick, Anthony, 11
Universal McCann, 29–30, 31
UX (user experience design), 9n

V
validation, internal, 14
value
    creating, 72, 127–128
    delivering, 66
    perceived, 130
value appropriation, 127–129

value chain, 121
value-added objectives, 135–137
value-added service, 126–127
viability, establishing, 122–123
Vigen, Tyler, 38
Voltaire, 61
vulnerabilities, exposing, 147

W
Waite, Jeremy, 95
Wald, Abraham, 12–13
Walker Information, 8
Wall Street Journal, 6
Walmart, 36
wants, 15, 31
webinars, 89
Welch, Jack, 76
Wells Fargo, 29
"what", 104, 107–108, 109, 113. *See
    also* 3W Ideation process
Whole Foods, 77
"why", 7, 80, 104, 106–107, 108,
    109, 113. *See also* context; 3W
    Ideation process
Why and Wherefore Statement,
    40–41
wisdom, 37, 89
workshops, 115. *See also* 3W
    Ideation process
Wow hypothesis, 104, 108–112. *See
    also* 3W Ideation process
    developing, 108–110
    example of, 109, 114
    verifying, 110–112, 114–115, 122

Z
Zabriskie, Kate, 17
Zaltman, Gerald, 19
Zhao, King, 1

ABOUT THE AUTHOR

Andrea began her career at a tech start-up fresh out of college. Learning on the fly and without a net, she helped build a company from $10,000 in seed money to a multimillion–dollar organization in only eight years.

In that time, she learned everything essential to grow a successful business, from sales to coding to accounting. Andrea then moved into a new role as the first female corporate executive at a $700 million global manufacturing company, leading digital strategy, marketing, and communications.

Managing ten business units across twelve countries garnered her the opportunity to study customer behavior across cultures. This sparked her focus on research and study in the burgeoning field of behavioral economics.

Over the next ten years, Andrea continued to expand her education, including at the University of Toronto and the Rochester Institute of Technology, building on her foundations in psychology and communications at the University of Iowa.

Founding the first customer-centricity and behavioral economics consulting firm in Iowa, she now works with a wide range of organizations across the financial, insurance, nonprofit, and A/C/E industries. Her work has spawned three books, more than one hundred published articles, and four contributing author roles.

She invented the 3W Ideation® process for identifying undiscovered needs by studying customer context, motivators, and biases.

Andrea also is the executive producer of two TEDx programs in the Midwest, and serves as a speaker coach and consultant for other TEDx programs across the country.